The
Conversation

———— ❧ ————

The Conversation

How Black Men and Women
Can Build Loving, Trusting Relationships

HILL HARPER

GOTHAM BOOKS

GOTHAM BOOKS
Published by Penguin Group (USA) Inc.
375 Hudson Street, New York, New York 10014, U.S.A.
Penguin Group (Canada), 90 Eglinton Avenue East, Suite 700, Toronto, Ontario M4P 2Y3, Canada (a division of Pearson Penguin Canada Inc.); Penguin Books Ltd, 80 Strand, London WC2R 0RL, England; Penguin Ireland, 25 St Stephen's Green, Dublin 2, Ireland (a division of Penguin Books Ltd); Penguin Group (Australia), 250 Camberwell Road, Camberwell, Victoria 3124, Australia (a division of Pearson Australia Group Pty Ltd); Penguin Books India Pvt Ltd, 11 Community Centre, Panchsheel Park, New Delhi—110 017, India; Penguin Group (NZ), 67 Apollo Drive, Rosedale, North Shore 0632, New Zealand (a division of Pearson New Zealand Ltd); Penguin Books (South Africa) (Pty) Ltd, 24 Sturdee Avenue, Rosebank, Johannesburg 2196, South Africa

Penguin Books Ltd, Registered Offices: 80 Strand, London WC2R 0RL, England

Published by Gotham Books, a member of Penguin Group (USA) Inc.

First printing, September 2009
10 9 8 7 6 5 4 3

Copyright © 2009 by Hill Harper
All rights reserved

Gotham Books and the skyscraper logo are trademarks of Penguin Group (USA) Inc.

LIBRARY OF CONGRESS CATALOGING-IN-PUBLICATION DATA
Harper, Hill, 1966–
  The conversation: how Black men and women can build loving, trusting relationships / by Hill Harper.
     p.   cm.
  ISBN 978-1-592-40475-9 (hardcover)
  1. Man-woman relationships—United States—Psychological aspects.   2. Man-woman relationships—United States.   3. African American women—Attitudes.   4. African American men—Attitudes.   I. Title
  HQ801.H3277 2009
  306.81089'96073—dc22   2009019688

Printed in the United States of America
Set in Bembo
Designed by Spring Hoteling

❧

This book is dedicated in loving memory to my grandparents, Eugenia and Harold Hill and Lillie and Harry Harper.

Thank you for showing me what love, happiness, partnership, and family look like. May you rest in blessed peace.

CONTENTS

❧

It took 100 years to set Black women and men apart from each other, but it has happened and the question now before us is, What are we willing to do about it?

—Susan Taylor, *The State of Black America 2008: In the Black Woman's Voice*

Introduction:
The Crisis of Our Shared Destiny

—⚜—

We are all tied together . . . in a garment of mutual destiny.

—Dr. Martin Luther King, Jr.,
married to Coretta Scott King for fifteen years, until his assassination

I am in no way representing myself as an expert in relationships, but rather as a man on a journey, attempting to figure it all out for myself. This book details a far more personal journey than I have written about in the past. I have been traveling lately through the inner territories of male and female relationships: love, partnership, asking questions about marriage and family. On this journey, I have looked inward, asking the same questions of myself that I am asking of my community.

I have kept a journal for years, but there is a way that the positive feedback of talking beyond yourself—sending a message out into the world in the form of a book and having the response come back to you as a human wave rising up to receive your message and listen and respond to you—really changes your perspective. As I researched this book, I started out with a few things that seemed important to say. I ended up on the receiving end of the well of human wisdom.

Blacks have been harder hit than other communities and ethnic groups by a handful of social, economic, and political problems that have led to a tragic dissolution of our community—and the integrity of our families—in the past four decades. The statistics are shocking, but you can see it in any Black community in this nation.

I'm very concerned about what is happening to the Black family. I'm worried by what my community feels like these days. We are regressing. We made huge leaps forward in the sixties and seventies, but somehow we are not holding it together anymore. We are not taking good enough care of one another, and this fact is supported by the divorce rate in our community; the levels of single parenting and fathers not taking care of their babies; and the disproportionate way that drugs and violence afflict our urban communities.

Discussions about the decline of the Black family date back to the 1980s. In fact, in 1985 the National Council of Negro Women (NCNW) instituted their first annual Black Family Reunion Celebration in response to all the negative headlines and talk about the "vanishing Black family." Dr. Dorothy Height, the chair of the NCNW, intended for it to be a celebration of the Black family's traditions and values and an affirmation of its resilience. The NCNW's annual Black Family Reunion Celebration continues to draw hundreds of thousands of Black families from around this country and from all walks of life.

As Blacks, we have a proud and strong legacy of family. Historically, when there were obstacles to overcome, we relied on family. When there were victories to be shared, we brought them to our families. When there were wounds to be healed, we opened them up to our families.

Our families and extended families kept us connected to one another and kept us connected to a deeper part of ourselves. I am not saying that every Black family has become disjointed and no longer has a connection to their roots or their legacy. But if we take a look at the data about how few single Black men and women are building long-term relationships and creating two-parent households, the news is sobering. Whether we want to admit it or not, we are bearing witness to the extinction of the Black family. We are in the midst of a crisis.

In 1966, more than 84 percent of all Black children were being raised in two-parent households. In 2006, just forty years later, fewer than 33 percent of all Black children were being raised in two-parent households. That's a precipitous 51 percent decline. We could blame it on the change in attitudes about marriage over the past forty years, but that still would not explain why, in 2006, more than 80 percent of Asian American children, nearly 75 percent of White American children, and close to 70 percent of Latino American children were being raised in two-parent households.

This book is about me thinking out loud, but plenty of my friends—men and women—are asking themselves the same questions. These questions run in two directions: We look inward and wonder what we want and try to imagine the life that will make us happy, and we look outward and ask the question, Why is it so difficult? What is happening in my community that has made it so hard for women and men to find their way to each other? Why are there so few folks who manage to hold a marriage together even when they have finally found a person they love? I don't have a clue, but I am filled with the need to know. That is where you come in. I want to advance the dialogue between women and men. I know we can do much better than we have been doing. This book is my effort at raising the bar for us all. I am challenging all of you to ask yourself these questions.

I am going to take you on a journey, and I invite you to come with me as I do some soul-searching on behalf of myself and I hope our community. Now, maybe you will relate and maybe you won't, but I feel that this is an important endeavor. It has to start somewhere, so why not with me? I care enough to start this conversation.

Throughout this journey, I've been fortunate to connect with a variety of couples from many walks of life, each at different key stages in their relationships. They shared their most private, most intimate, most challenging experiences in the hope that their open discussions would inspire each of us to initiate and begin our own conversations. So with that said, if you don't like some of what you read, please don't shoot the messenger. I am going to be brutally truthful throughout this entire journey we are about to take together.

Now that you have been officially warned about the honesty you can expect, let me back up a bit and share with you how we got here in the first place. One by one, group by group, state by state, e-mail to e-mail, phone call to phone call, lunch to brunch, brunch to dinner, dinner to the club, I have gathered with men and women—some friends and some strangers; some married, some divorced, and some single—and with all of them I have had conversations: intimate conversations, personal conversations, revealing conversations.

My conversation partners have included men and women who trusted me enough to expose private struggles, past pains, emotional vulnerabilities, real concerns, and often unaddressed mis-understandings that continue to plague Black men, Black women, and our relationships. They are not celebrities offering glamor-ized versions of their relationship successes and struggles, but rather everyday folks in real relationships, doing their best to live truly happy lives. As you will see, some are finding more success achieving that goal than others. Where I fit in that continuum will become very clear as you read on. Unlike the version of the book I first envisioned—me gathering information and sharing it with you—in this book you'll find that my life took an un-expected turn and changed that idea. You see, along the way I started to recognize myself in other peoples' stories and struggles and came to understand that like so many others, I am also in my own repetitive cycle.

As you read this book, you may at times gasp; you may be shocked, surprised, embarrassed, insulted, and otherwise offended by some of its content. I've included elements that push buttons because with male-female conversations in our community, it seems in many ways that it's what *we're not saying* that is contribut-ing to the demise of our relationships. For all our sakes, it's time to make that push so that we can get unstuck out of our comfort zone and move back into the power position as a successful community. I want the book to follow in form and substance what needs to happen in our interpersonal relationships—no-holds-barred com-munication. That is truly what *The Conversation* is about. To have completely, embarrassingly honest conversations takes courage. *Courage* is one of my favorite words. The etymology of the word is *cor*, meaning "heart." Speaking from the heart means truly being able to speak about *all* things that are in you, and then, in turn, living from your heart. Most people have been taught to live from their heads, which is what people who have had to survive have learned how to do. But at this point in our journey, if we stay in that place we will bear witness to our own destruction—all the while playing it safe and blaming one another.

When I talk with my male and female friends, one thing I keep hearing is just how angry and distrustful women and men are of each other. That really saddens me. I do not believe we are so far away from each other that we can't find our way back to peace. But I do not even know why the war started, so this book is also an investigation. It is questions mixed with thoughts and the answers I have been able to find as I try to get to the heart of the matter.

I'm sharing this journey, and the lessons I've learned while on it, in hopes of inspiring all of us to communicate with one another. In so doing, I hope we can reintroduce ourselves. I hope that in the conversation we can become friends again, because we are— all of us—the newest, best, most perfect model of human being. And we all deserve to be *unreasonably happy*.

In the course of this book, I am going to attempt to achieve a deeper understanding of myself and of the world I am living in. I am calling this book *The Conversation* because my hope is that these words that originate with me at my laptop will find their way to the book in your hands, pushing you and inspiring you to talk with your friends and families. I hope eventually to extend that dialogue across the barricades that men and women have erected to protect themselves from each other. We are growing jaded, cynical, tired, and world-weary before our time. We are expecting less and demanding less, and those lower expectations are making us unfulfilled and taking us farther from each other. The walls between us do not serve us. I would love to see women talking to and asking questions of men, and vice versa, to bring more clarity and peace to the way we deal with each other. Why? Because some way, somehow, there needs to be communion between us. I want us to figure out how we got to this place so we can retrace our steps back to the time when there was trust between us.

What this book is about is plumbing our own depths and figuring out what relationship and love and endurance and commitment mean to all of us, and then planting our flag on that ground so we can begin to live there and build our lives there.

If we can figure out for ourselves how to reach that destination, then and only then can we start to create large numbers of healthy loving relationships and two-parent families. This is no small thing. Our children will know enduring love because they will be born on this fertile ground. This is an invaluable gift we can provide to the next generation, and they deserve better than the landscape we are currently offering. If I can do this, and you can do this, then we can represent love in such an elevated and fierce way that everyone we know wants some of what we've got, and we can change what the past four decades of shrinking Black relationships suggests is our destiny.

I believe that finding good relationships means first giving good love to ourselves. And I believe that when we give good love to ourselves, we will not settle for less than a righteous and fulfilling relationship. So it is a circle. As you give love out, it's received and reciprocated—and it grows. That's the beauty of it. Love is an energy. You can feed it to people, and they, in turn, feed it to others, and eventually it comes back to nurture you.

I am stepping into the circle because I want to learn the lessons I will find there. In this circle, we must decide whether we are willing to have the courage to do battle for a new future, and in so doing, realize that the battle is to tame our own hearts and to allow ourselves to be loved. We're going to reach down through the ages to the warrior-queens and kings of our African past and do battle. We will corral ourselves and fight with ourselves and train ourselves to be warriors for love who know how to commit, to follow through, and to raise strong children who speak the languages of love and family and emotional security. And when we win these battles, we will be better and stronger and the world will say, "Amen."

C'mon, jump into the circle. Your heart demands nothing less. Let's start *The Conversation*.

PART I:
THE CONVERSATION BEGINS

FROM THE DESK OF HILL HARPER

6/3

- I wanna have kids and I want my kids to have two parents under the same roof.

- A lotta dates, still (LONELY.)

- I want to feel head over heels in love. I want to feel my heart beating faster.

~~I need~~

- Being out there has gotten old. No doubt have I come to want something that's more real – easier said than done.

- My grandparents built lives together. They committed to their commitment to each other. Do I have the courage to do that with somebody??

1.

Man in the Mirror

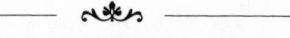

We need more light about each other. Light creates understanding,
understanding creates love, love creates patience, and patience creates unity.

—Malcolm X,
married to Betty Shabazz for seven years, until his assassination

The simple yet profound act of holding a mirror up to yourself can truly be a frightening experience. It's as if you're seeing yourself through new eyes. While most parts may seem familiar, you begin to notice new things about yourself that are unrecognizable—utterly foreign—that make you feel as though you're staring at a complete stranger.

That is what I wound up contending with earlier this year as I caught a glimpse of myself in my car's rearview mirror. I was in Washington, D.C., on a rainy night, driving back to my hotel after attending a party that had left me feeling somewhat confused and despondent about my life—more specifically, about the fact that I'm still single. I was making a mental list of explanations and excuses for why I have failed to maintain any sort of long-term relationship over these past twenty years of so-called adult life. Those reasons went from the petty to the profoundly inane, from "I honestly don't have the time to devote to a relationship" to "All the amazing women are already married." After each one I'd nod and hear myself saying, "Yeah, that's right," as if I was trying to convince myself that it was fact, that the solution had to be out of my control because, after all, I wasn't to blame; I was a victim of circumstance.

I was stopped at a streetlight when I came to that brilliant conclusion. As the light changed from red to green I glanced in the rearview mirror, as I had done at least a dozen times already that night on my journey back to the hotel. For the first time since I don't even know when, I saw myself. I held my own gaze long enough for me to see past the deception, past all those clever excuses and disguises; I *saw* me. "Who do you think you're fooling?" I asked aloud. "Of course you're part of the problem." Then the driver behind me blew his horn, snapping me out of my honesty, forcing me to focus on the road again.

I start with this moment because for me it symbolizes both a beginning and an end. Seeing myself, my truer self, I didn't want to go back to that old vision—that old version—of me. It's like those optical illusions: Once your eyes settle on a shape in an image—the bird in flight, the clock with its hands at three P.M., the profile of a woman's face—you'll never again see that picture as a random series of dots. You can't un-see what you've seen and return it to the way it used to be. You can only move forward and search for whatever else exists in the picture. But first, I have to explain what happened before. I have to tell you how I found myself driving down that street evaluating the state of my love life—or lack thereof.

Earlier that day, I delivered a keynote speech at a conference in Washington, D.C. My friend Don Watkins stopped by afterward. The two of us go way back; we've been buddies since high school. Though over the years we'd usually done a good job of staying in touch, Don and I hadn't really talked or seen each other in about three years. He'd heard that I was going to be in town and decided to show up and be that familiar face in the crowd for me. After my speech, we sat in a coffee shop talking smack, trying to catch up on each other's lives. The time flew by. We'd been talking for what felt like two minutes—it was really two hours—when Don realized he was late for a prior engagement. He and his wife, Robin, were attending a small dinner celebration for her parents' fiftieth wedding anniversary.

"Hill, why don't you just come along?" he asked. I hesitated for a second, but then said yes. I wasn't home; I didn't have any other plans, and besides, I couldn't very well say no without looking and feeling like a complete jerk.

Don and Robin got married right out of college. They'd met during freshman year, started dating, and fell senselessly in love. I remember when Don decided to ask Robin to marry him. I was home on Christmas break and a bunch of us guys were hanging out. When he broke the news, the whole room fell silent. Then everybody suddenly busted out laughing. We thought for sure Don had lost his mind. Marriage?! We were barely in our twenties. There was still so much more time. There were still so many more women. He hadn't even really dated anybody else—not since high school, and not for any impressive length of time. Now he was going to take a vow. He was going to promise to be with Robin forever.

"You do realize that forever is an unimaginable length of time?" I overheard Robin's father, Mr. Blake, asking as I walked into his wife, Hattie's, living room. There were fewer than two dozen people there, some of them standing by the bar fixing drinks. Most of them were seated near the fireplace on sofas and ottomans, engaged in what seemed to be a lively conversation.

I walked over to Robin's parents, Foster and Hattie Blake, greeted them, and gave them my gift, a bottle of champagne. Don brought me a drink, and Robin introduced me to the entire room. There were six couples: one was young, thirtysomething, and the other three were the Blakes' contemporaries, septuagenarians who'd been married for longer than I'd been alive. Scattered among all that wedded bliss were five unpartnered people—four women and one man, me.

"Have a seat, son," Mr. Blake said to me, holding his hand out in the direction of a vacant ottoman. I liked the way he called me *son*. Between the familial warmth of that address and the literal warmth generated by the fireplace, I immediately felt at home. "We were in the middle of talking about history, about how some of us here have learned that you should never say *never*."

"But you have to admit it *was* an unimaginable event," insisted Doc Mayweather setting his plate of food down on the coffee table. "I never would've even dared to dream it." His wife, Miss Brenda, who was sitting next to him, nodded. "Mmm-hmmm," she added. "Who'd have thought we could ever achieve something like that?" It took me a minute to figure out that they were talking about politics, not relationships. The older folks had been talking about how they still couldn't believe that our country had elected a Black man as president. None of them had thought it would happen in their lifetime.

"And that wife of his." Miss Brenda smiled. "She is quite a woman."

"Says a lot about him that he knew not to just pass her by," said a distinguished-looking man whose name I hadn't caught. He and his wife looked so much like Ruby Dee and the late Ossie Davis, I kept doing double takes.

"Uh-huh," his wife agreed. "Says a lot about her that she's not afraid to stand behind her man."

"That's 'cause she's confident in her own intelligence and education," Miss Brenda added. "She knows it doesn't take anything away from her."

"You can say that again," Mr. Blake said, reaching for Mrs. Blake's hand. "That's the problem with you young brothers and sisters today. It's always me, me, me, me, me; always about the individual and so rarely about the community. No wonder the Black family is just falling apart."

"Can't see the worth in it enough to sacrifice for it." Doc Mayweather frowned. Whereas before, they were just having a general conversation, now they seemed to be talking directly to us, at us, the single ones in the group.

"I sure hope," Doc Mayweather continued, "you young people . . ."

Just then, the woman who was seated on the ottoman next to mine leaned over and asked if I wanted to go with her to the dining room to fix myself a plate of food. I said yes, happy for the chance to escape the lecture that was clearly on its way.

Her name was Nichole, and she was drop-dead gorgeous. I followed her in a slow circle as we filled our plates with food from the several platters that had been set buffet style on the table. We chatted as we scooped. Once we'd each answered the obligatory "So, how do you know the Blakes?" question, we moved on to more personal topics. Nichole had majored in math at Howard and now taught calculus in the D.C. public schools.

"Calculus?" I asked in disbelief. It'd been ages since I'd thought of integers, derivatives, and L'Hospital's rule. They were high on the list of things I was glad to forget once I'd graduated high school. Nichole just smiled. She was used to that response. She went and leaned against the wall where the dining room ended and the living room began. I followed and stood beside her, and we continued our conversation. Soon we had turned toward each other as we talked.

The energy between us was palpable. I don't know whether it was because we'd been sitting in that room full of all those couples, but we gravitated toward each other in a way that was almost effortless. There wasn't any strained laughter or shyness, and there weren't any awkward moments, not even when she told me that she had an adolescent daughter. The conversation simply flowed.

"She's with her father this weekend." Nichole voluntarily explained that she and her daughter's father had never been married and that their coparenting relationship was difficult and contentious at times. "Do you have any kids?" she asked.

"Not yet," I replied. Before she could respond, Mr. Blake called out to me:

"Son, would you mind bringing me a few of those wings? The ones with the hot sauce . . . not the wimpy ones the Mayweathers brought."

Nichole followed me back into the living room when I brought Mr. Blake the plate I'd fixed for him. The group was still talking about the state of the Black family. Nichole and I sat down and listened, stealing a glance or a smile at each other every now and then. I looked around the room at all the couples and how connected they were, literally. There were clasped hands, or hands resting on thighs, just above the bended knee, or gently rubbing backs and shoulders. I was filled with both an inexplicable joy and an immeasurable sadness. Both emotions led me to my grandparents, all four of whom would have fit in perfectly with this group. A group I admired but felt strangely at odds with.

"I should get going," I blurted out. "I've got an early day tomorrow."

"See what I mean?" Doc Mayweather chuckled. "These young'uns today. They're always running around, going here and there, doing this and that. How're you supposed to settle down into a life when you can't even sit still for a night?" Everyone laughed at that, even me.

Don walked with me outside. By the time we got to my rental car, the inexplicable joy I was feeling a few minutes earlier had all but disappeared, leaving only sadness and confusion. As I approached the car door, about to drive away from all that love and laughter, I think I felt lonelier than I had at any other time in my life. "Where is my partner? Where is my true love?" are the questions that were swimming around in my head.

"All right, then, tomorrow," Don said, referring to the plans we'd just made to finish our catch-up session. When I pulled the car key out of my pocket, a little slip of paper flew out with it. I shoved it back into my pocket, got into the car, and started to drive. I thought about the neat, cursive writing on the paper, and about the numbers and hyphens, all so perfectly aligned, as if they were a part of an equation.

"Will you call?" Nichole had asked when she'd handed me the paper. The vulnerability in her voice was endearing. It made me feel protective of her. I told her I would, and that was the truth. I'd probably wait until I was back at home, in Los Angeles, to give her a call. By then, we'd both be questioning whatever it was that had passed between us, whether it was real or imagined. Even if we decided that it was real, we'd be too far away from it for that to mean anything, or make any difference.

Nichole was the kind of woman that men dream of meeting. She was beautiful, inside and out, smart, witty, direct, and self-possessed, but still vulnerable underneath it all. She was going to make some man very happy—but deep down I knew that man wasn't going to be me. What I didn't understand was: *Why not?*

At that very moment, alone in my rental car, for reasons I can't explain, my mind flashed to nine years earlier. The memory was me sitting in the hospital, at the side of my father's bed as he battled cancer. I remembered him telling me, with tears in his eyes, that his biggest regret his entire life was that he didn't make it work with my mother. "We should have stayed partnered," he said sadly. Twelve hours later I cried, prayed, and held his hand as my brother and I helplessly watched him die. Staying partnered in my family has seemingly ended with his parents.

My grandparents anchored our family. They reminded us of who we were, where we came from, and showed us where we might go. Both sets of my grandparents were married more than fifty years. They were truly partners and invited the family into their circle. As a boy, I remember attending family reunions each year for both sides of my family, the Hills and the Harpers, in South Carolina and Iowa, respectively. Each reunion was com-memorated by a T-shirt bearing a photograph of the family, with the day and year of the event printed below it. My grandparents hosted almost every family reunion.

Much like that evening at the Blakes', those reunions drew us together. I loved them, mainly because it made me feel like I was a part of something larger, a network of people. There were the cousins, some of whom were so far removed that it would take pen and paper to figure out exactly where and how our blood-lines crossed. And then, of course, there were the "cousins" who we knew were not related to us by blood, but were still kin. A lot of us grew up attending family reunions like those. They allowed us to connect, to know one another and experience why family is so valuable.

The Hill and Harper families no longer hold yearly reunions. Last year, through a family-wide e-mail, we were all informed that the final Iowa Harper family reunion would take place in Fort Madison, next to my grandfather's farm. As a child, I spent almost every summer at that farm. Even now I can close my eyes and recall every inch and acre of that land and the memories that they hold. When my grandparents passed, the farm was sold, making it virtually impossible to hold any more family reunions on that property.

A couple of years ago, I bought thirty-seven acres of land in Colorado, along the Roaring Fork River. I thought, in my own deluded way, that I was trying to address the problem. I envisioned myself building a house on that land, a place where my own family reunions could take place. I wanted to emulate, if not duplicate, for my future children and grandchildren, what my grandparents had given me. But the truth of the matter is that love is not about places; it's about people. If I can't get it together to create a family, there will be no family to reunite. Deep down, I knew that. My grandparents were such a powerful force in our family because of the love they shared with us and with each other. It was sustaining. I feel blessed that I was able to witness and share in the stability of their love and way of life because, in my family at least, it seemed to end with their generation. My parents divorced when I was six years old, and much to my fear and frustration, the older I get the more and more elusive marriage seems to become.

The elders at the Blakes' party weren't wrong when they talked about the demise of the Black family. Since the first slave ships docked in Jamestown, Virginia, Blacks have understood the connection between the past, the present, and the future. Without our history there's no path forward. Seemingly only the most recent generations have forgotten that you can't write your future without revering your past. There had never been a time when we did not realize that the basic foundation of the Black family was under attack. From the raping of women and the lynching of men, to Jim Crow and the Tuskegee experiments, through the passage of the "man-in-the-house rule," which denied welfare and social services to families that had adult men in the household—a law that basically encouraged fathers to be absent—Black men and Black women stayed connected. But sometime during the past forty years those connections have frayed. Maybe we've decided that life would be less burdensome if we weren't tethered to one another. Some people say that it was because of integration. That once we were able to move away from the neighborhood, the physical community, we turned our backs on one another and on all the emotional commitments and responsibilities we had to our communities. What a painful idea to consider.

For so many of us, Barack and Michelle Obama are calming and hope-inspiring representatives of our future partly because they are reminders of our past, of the Black family's ability to survive, succeed, and ultimately triumph. They provide hope that marriage of the sort that our grandparents and their grandparents had is not only within reach but can be free of the acrimony, abuse, neglect, dishonesty, competition, and professional jealousy we've grown accustomed to encountering in our modern relationships.

Whatever their romantic struggles, neither of the Obamas set their eyes on the White House when they first envisioned themselves in a happy and healthy committed relationship. By buying that property in Colorado, I was putting the cart before the horse. I was thinking I could buy a property to house my memories and build a family before I had even done the work of creating relationships and experiences worthy of remembering.

I think we all know much more about ourselves than we care to admit. If we were honest, we would be forced to acknowledge we are not making the most of our present; or the best choices for our future. Most of us are addicted to our patterns. I know I am: relationships, food, friends, shopping, spirituality, credit cards, family, and on and on. We get habitual. I justify my patterned behavior by saying "Well, that's just who I am." Really? Talk about not looking in the mirror.

That's why that moment in the car was so significant. In it's rearview mirror I saw myself. I saw my patterns. I saw my fears that keep me in those patterns. I knew that if I didn't want my relationships to keep going the way they had been, I would have to change. If I want just a little bit of what my grandparents had I would have to make different choices. The images of my father, my grandparents, the Blakes, Nichole, and Don and Robin kept swimming in my head.

There was a part of me that wanted to turn around, drive back to the Blakes', and see whether Nichole was still there. I have no idea what I would have said to her but that's not as important as the fact that I didn't go back. As quickly as my newfound resolve came, my same old habit-filled excuses returned—in this case quicker than usual: "Come on, Hill, you're too tired to go anywhere except back to the hotel room." I had thought and felt myself right into exhaustion. I needed time to process it all, to figure out what it all meant and how to proceed. Only then would I be able to take what I knew would be the next step.

I'm ready now.

2.

What We Say, Mean, and Do

Well, the truth about life is that we're all alone, but when somebody loves you, right, that experience is shared. Love is the only real connective tissue that allows you to not live and die by yourself. It gives you purpose beyond you.

—Will Smith,
married to Jada Pinkett Smith since 1997

There seems to be an overriding belief among some people that men and women are so vastly different that it is almost impossible for us to truly communicate with each other. I was watching an old Chris Rock stand-up routine, and with his distinctive, singsongy voice, he said, "There are only three things women need in life: food, water, and compliments!" Now, Chris has been married to his lovely wife, Malaak, for a number of years, and, yes, he was joking, but there is always some truth in comedy. Is this how a lot of men really think? Or do men think the opposite: that women are extremely complicated? What do sisters really want and need? How can we as men begin to understand them?

Most of my friends—both men and women—fundamentally want the same thing. They want to be happy, healthy, successful, and loved. Now, there is no doubt that men and women tend to approach life in different ways. My guy friends are much more simplistic in many ways than my female friends. But that may have more to do with the way men and women are socialized than with what our true desires are. It made me wonder how couples manage to make it work at all, if we start off with such apparently uneven perspectives.

The first image that flashed through my mind was of me sitting on that ottoman in the Blakes' living room. I thought of all those couples and of how long they'd been married. The older couples were finishing each other's sentences, eating off each other's plates. That's the kind of companionship my friends always tell me they want to have. It's definitely the kind I hope to have one day. Looking at and listening to those couples, it's pretty easy to attribute their closeness and comfort with each other to the longevity of their relationships. But obviously it has to be about more than how many years they've been together. Time can't guarantee the growth of something that doesn't exist. The foundational elements for what they now share had to have been in place at the beginning of their relationship. You don't suddenly find yourself finishing your wife's sentences if you've been ignoring her most important feelings for the better part of fifty years.

I know that relationships take work. And I don't want to over-romanticize the fact that we are not *always* going to enjoy being around the same person day after day, year after year. I wondered what the relationship between Mr. and Mrs. Blake might have looked like fifty years earlier, when they first met. Had he always enjoyed listening to her? Had she known right away that he would be what she wanted? If their daughter Robin's courtship with my boy Don was similar in any way, then the answer to both questions is yes. When I finally met Robin, I felt like I already knew her so well. Every time I had talked to Don he'd tell me about something Robin did or what her perspective on what we were talking about was. At first I thought it was a little much, but after a few months, I began to really admire how important her opinions were to him, and how seriously he took her ideas . . . and vice versa. Don't get me wrong; it wasn't as if they were perfect. They disagreed, and they had their fair share of problems, but a lack of consideration wasn't one of them.

Nichole also came to my mind. Since I've committed to being honest in these pages, I'll go ahead and admit that thinking about the Blakes and the other couples prompted me to imagine myself with Nichole in fifty years. (Yes, I'm man enough to admit that guys let their minds wander to fantasyland, too . . . though truth be told, our fantasies more often involve thongs and teddies . . . but I digress.) Nichole had been so easy to talk to, to listen to. Everything felt so comfortable. I'm sure the atmosphere had something to do with it. I liked the fact that the flirtation between us wasn't so overt that it got in the way of either one of us being ourselves.

But then I hadn't called her that night. Or the next day. Or the next. Even though I really liked her, it took me a whole month to call her. That piece of paper she'd written her number on sat by the phone on my desk the entire time. I would look at it and ask myself, "What does she want?" Was she looking for a man who was husband material? What about her daughter? What relationship was the man in her life expected to have with her? Did she want more children? And then there was the obvious question of location. Was she looking for a man who would adjust his life to accommodate hers, or would she be willing to adjust her life and relocate if she met the right man? Or did she just want an easy, breezy affair with weekend rendezvous in exotic locations and the occasional movie premiere?

When we were standing there in the dining room talking, none of these questions came to mind. I didn't consider for a moment that she wanted anything other than what we had right there. We were becoming friends, getting to know each other, and that seemed to be enough for both of us. By the time I called her, just as I'd predicted (and maybe even wanted on some level), whatever connection we'd had between us was broken, betrayed by my lengthy silence. It was a surface-level polite conversation that ended with me saying, "Okay, great speaking with you. Talk to you soon." It sounded like I was saying good-bye to my accountant.

Why did I wait so long to call her? Fear? Self-sabotage? I don't know. I do know that when I get caught up, trying to figure out what a woman might want from me, I shut down: I get trapped in my head, and part of me becomes anxious and scared. I let my fears say, "Oh, it's not worth it. . . . She's probably not 'the one' anyway. . . . You meet tons of women, so what difference does it make?" Maybe deep down, especially if I like her, I'm afraid I won't be able to meet her expectations. Or she won't meet mine. Or maybe I'm simply afraid of getting hurt.

I know I shouldn't, but in the past, I've put friendship and romance in two different categories. Friendships have limitations and expectations. When I know that I'm friends with a woman, I feel more at ease because I can trust those boundaries. With friendship, intentions, words, and actions are more often in alignment. In potentially romantic relationships, I feel like there is a greater risk of falling prey to someone else's agenda.

It seemed like I was on my way to repeating my same old patterns with Nichole. Maybe it's a guy thing. As irrational as it may sound, it seems men always want to believe that we have everything figured out, even if it's obvious that we don't. When I was waiting to call Nichole, I was acting as if I needed to know exactly what a woman wanted before I would even think about opening up to her. I've made that mistake before, and I believe it has affected many of my relationships. But admitting I don't have everything figured out is the best progress that I've made in a while.

So to try to help me figure out my relationship issues, I called one of my best girlfriends, Julia. To be clear, Julia has plenty of relationship issues of her own, but I've known her for years and she has had a clear view of me and of how I've been with the women I've dated. We decided to have lunch, and I told her about my experiences at the Blakes' and in D.C. Julia offered a very simple and blunt explanation: "Hill, you're emotionally unavailable . . . that's your problem, and the problem with most men!"

Emotionally unavailable? Me? Those were the last words I thought anybody would ever use to describe me. I mean, I knew I was as flawed as the next person, but I also believed that my emotions were pretty damn available. It was a necessary part of my profession. Acting is all about putting your emotions out in the open, standing center stage with them.

Acting aside, I'd written two mentoring books, one for young men and the other for young women. Both are epistolary, in the tradition of Rilke. In the letters, I share my own experiences, some of which are extremely personal. How could someone describe me as emotionally unavailable?

Julia was so specific in her assessment. She didn't bother with the simplistic characterization lobbed at many men, saying I was a "commitment-phobe." That explanation is usually the easy way out used by men and women to cover up underlying issues. Julia reiterated, "You are emotionally unavailable."

"You are absolutely one of the most sensitive men I know," Julia consoled me, "with your friends and with your fans. But I've known you long enough to have noticed that emotionally, you're more distant, more removed, from the women you're romantically involved with. It's almost as if you don't want to give up too much of yourself or let them get too close to you. So, what you say, what you mean, and what you do are all different things with the women you meet." And then she concluded, "Hill, I love you like a brother, but just like a lot of men, you are full of shit."

"What!? Come on. That's not true," I protested. A part of me knew that it was, but I didn't want it to be true. I wasn't even sure why I created that emotional distance, but I knew that I did. Another thing I knew: I wasn't alone in that practice.

I've had the opportunity and privilege, traveling around the country during my book tours and speaking engagements, to meet and talk to many amazing people—young men and women, executives and professionals, intellectuals, and just everyday folks. Whether it's because they've read my books or because they've seen me in a film or on TV, a lot of them trust me and feel comfortable enough with me to share their feelings and personal experiences. It was through those interactions that I started to wonder whether men and women even talk to each other. I mean really talk—easily and freely, without reservation—like we do with our friends. I even started to wonder whether men and women considered each other friends, or if we automatically compartmentalized our relationships: We're either lovers or we're platonic friends, but not both. Truth be told, the comments I heard made me wonder—despite all the emphatic "I *love* men" and "I *love* women" declarations—whether men and women really even liked each other at all.

So many women seem to be mistrustful of men, and so many men seem suspicious of women. It is as if the romantic relationships between men and women exist in three parallel worlds—the world of what is said, the world of what is meant, and the world of what is done, and rarely are the three in any sort of alignment. For example: what he said: "I love you"; what he meant: "I love you in this moment"; what he did: not call for a few days. Or another example:

What is said: "I'll try and call you tonight and maybe we'll get together."
What is meant: "You're not my first choice so if that falls through I'll call."
What is done: He shows up at midnight, has sex, stays a few hours, and leaves.

Like so many people, I existed comfortably in all of those misaligned worlds. It's what I had grown accustomed to. It's how many single people (men *and* women) dole out the truth and negotiate intimacy, especially with people they suspect are not "the one," assuming they believe the idea of "the one" is real at all. It isn't about misleading or hurting anybody, but sometimes dealing with people in those parallel worlds feels almost safe. Neither person has to reveal anything about his or her true self. So how could

I ever truly become close to someone I was dating if she could never get to know the real me and I never got to see the real her?

For instance, why would you talk to someone you're seeing about marriage if you think that doesn't exist in the foreseeable future of your relationship? What would be the point in telling your partner what you want from a marriage, or the ways you've thought of getting married? Likewise, does your partner have to mention that she is seriously entertaining the possibility of relocating in six months if she does not believe you will still be a significant other in her life then?

As Julia got her car from the valet, she could tell that I was still somewhat shell-shocked by our lunch. Over her shoulder she yelled, "You need to develop a real relationship, Hill." Yeah, easier said than done.

The person with the most "real" relationship I knew was Don. So as I drove away from my lunch with Julia, licking my wounds, I grabbed my cell and called him. Don has been with Robin for two decades. It still is amazing to me that he can say he's been married for almost twenty years. I think back through all of the things I've been through over the past twenty years, and I think, *They were married through all that.* I wondered whether what was going on in the head of a married man my age was very different from my perspective as a single man. Don didn't answer, so I left him a long voice mail and asked him to either call or e-mail me. What I didn't think about at the time was that one of the secrets of their marriage is communication, and when Robin heard that Don was answering these questions for me, she wanted to offer her response as well.

> One of the secrets of marriage is communication.

The basic gist of my voice mail to Don was this: "As a man who's been married for most of your life, what would you say is the biggest challenge facing Black relationships?"

RESPONSE FROM DON

Hi, Hill.

I've been thinking a lot about some of the stuff we discussed over dinner last week. Here's the story of how Robin and I got together and how we've been able to make our commitment to each other last. My version of it, that is.

Robin and I met during our freshman year of college. She was fine, and she had style, and I had every intention of getting to know her, but I was not looking for a long-term committed relationship. First year of college is spread-your-wings time. Until then, the longest relationship I'd ever been in was six months, and I had no intention of breaking that record. Twenty years later, here I am happily married to the same woman. We've been together for more than half of our lives. Shows what I knew back then.

I've had plenty of people ask me what the formula is. To be honest, in many ways I think we got lucky, or as we prefer to say—we were blessed. Sure I'd love to wax poetic about things like hard work, communication, compromise, and keeping romance alive, but the truth is, I didn't think about any of those things when I got married. My wife and I laugh about how we thought we knew everything when we walked down the aisle at twenty and twenty-one years old. The longer we were married, the more we realized how little we knew about relationships. We've basically had to learn on the job, but there is one thing we did from the beginning that I know has made a difference. From day one, we declared our love as special, and committed ourselves to fiercely defending that claim against anything or anyone who dared to challenge it.

I've been thinking a lot about the question you asked: What is the biggest challenge that is facing Black relationships? I'm not really sure how to answer it, but here's my best attempt.

Every relationship is going to be tested. The pressures of society are numerous and well documented. You have jealous people who want what you have (a committed, loving relationship), and if they can't take it, they will settle for destroying it. Then, of course, our own individual differences can sometimes pose a huge threat to a relationship. But these aren't particularly unique or major problems. They are common hurdles that any relationship must eventually overcome. Black relationships, however, must contend with a set of very specific obstacles, including one I think is the most difficult of all to overcome.

I asked my wife the same question that you asked of me, and she came to the same conclusion without knowing what my answer was going to be. The biggest challenge to Black love relationships is our fear of each other. All Black relationships are affected, to some degree, by the long-festering insecurities we have about the opposite sex, insecurities that are specific to Black Americans for

> ∽
> **The biggest challenge to love is fear.**
> ∽

a number of reasons. We all know how the song goes: Black men are no-good, lazy, shiftless, womanizing, disrespectful dogs, put on Earth for the sole purpose of abusing the Black woman and taking her for granted. Black women are overbearing, overdemanding, nagging, money-hungry bitches, put on Earth for the sole purpose of emasculating the Black man and making sure he knows they don't need him. I won't go into too much detail about how and why Black love is under so much pressure, because I think most of us have heard it before.

After twenty years of marriage, expert or not, I will stand before you and state without qualification: If you think the negative effects of our history will not have an effect on you and your relationships, you are wrong. I want you to know you're wrong, because I want you to be ready for it.

If you're like I was, you consider yourself part of a new, enlightened generation that can easily shed the baggage of our past and usher in a new era of Black love. I saw the hurtful stereotypes and misperceptions for what they were, and I condemned them. As an educated, forward-thinking Black man, I vowed to never fall prey to them. And I have to say, in a rational state of mind, I probably would have had no problem keeping that vow. Unfortunately, when it comes to romantic relationships, most of us spend our time in an irrational state of mind.

As I'm sure you already know, Hill, where emotions rule, logic is often lacking. You may think you're untainted by the old hang-ups that have plagued Black relationships for generations, but I doubt it. One day, you may find yourself in a sour mood as your lady walks into the bathroom and innocently reminds you to put the cap back on the toothpaste, and suddenly out of nowhere, you blurt out, "Stop trying to control me!"

A number of episodes like that quickly brought my wife and me out of denial. We realized that our relationship would inevitably be played out against the backdrop of our historical legacy. We each had our share of inherited cultural and historical baggage, and we would have to learn to cope with it, the same *way we've coped with issues over money, spirituality, and child rearing, the differences being that those other issues were expected. Having to deal with the baggage of the Black American experience caught us completely by surprise. At times our reactions to things were motivated by fears so deeply rooted in our subconscious, we couldn't even stop ourselves from feeling them.*

It all stems from the fear we have that one day the person we've chosen to love may turn out to be a "typical" Black man or woman. And as much as we'd like to believe we haven't bought into those stereotypes, they are there. That's why we tend to take individual behavior and use it to condemn the group, either Black men or women. I don't have the solution for making that fear go away; I just know it's there.

Hill, do not make the mistake of thinking you're too enlightened to let the horrific past of Black America seep into your relationships. Extreme conditions produce extreme reactions that may be appropriate, or even necessary

> ❧
> ## Stick it out.
> ❧

in the moment, but they continue long after the conditions that caused them have passed. I didn't experience the Great Depression, but to this day, I find myself saving table scraps. Notice, I didn't say leftovers. I said table scraps, like a pinkie-sized crumb of bread. And you know what, Hill? Those scraps never get eaten, but I don't feel right just throwing them away. So I put them in the refrigerator until they become inedible. I know it doesn't make sense, but I do it out of habit, because when I was a kid that's what my mother did. We talked about it when I got older. She told me saving everything was something her mother had passed on to her because she grew up during the Great Depression, when saving every bit of food was an act of survival. The Great Depression lasted less than fifteen years, but here I am, two generations later, wrapping half a green bean in aluminum foil. That's how deep patterns are. That's how deep social conditioning is.

I can only imagine how long Black Americans will be impacted by what we've endured over the past three hundred years. That is why I implore you to embrace this reality, Hill. If you accept that making any new relationship work will mean dealing with not only personal baggage but also the baggage of our legacy, you will be better prepared to deal with it. It's a lesson my wife and I learned early on and have kept in mind ever since. We know we can't eliminate the doubts and fears from flaring up from time to time, but we're able to identify them, deal with them, and get past them. In my mind, that is the key factor in sustaining Black love.

Hill, I know you just asked me to answer the question. You didn't ask for my advice, but I'm gonna give it to you anyway because this is the advice I give to all my single brothas, and just because you got two degrees from Harvard doesn't mean you're too smart to learn something. So here goes:

"You stick it out."

Hill, approach Black love the same way you'd approach taking a vacation to someplace hot, like Egypt. You've heard how great it is and you want to go. You've been looking forward to this trip your whole life. Of course, you're going to pack accordingly—shorts, tank tops, wide-brimmed hats, and maybe some sunblock. But even though you knew where you were going, you heard about the weather, and you came prepared, you still get caught off guard when you step off that plane. "Oh, Lord. I knew it was going to be hot; I didn't know it was going to be this hot." You like it hot, but somehow the idea of being *in that heat for an extended period of time feels suffocating, and a little scary. That first couple of days you might even wonder if you made a mistake, but you really want to see this historic beautiful place that everyone's been talking about, so you don't get back on the plane. You stick it out. That's what you have to do with love; you have to stick it out.*

A week later, it's still just as hot, but you don't mind anymore. You're used to it now. You don't even think about it. In fact, you like it hot. Your reward for staying is the chance to take in amazing sights you'll never forget; taste incredible foods you've never heard of before; go on remarkable adventures and learn things about yourself that leave you in a constant state of wonderment; you might even fancy yourself fluent in a new language. When it's time to leave, all you're able to think about is your next visit to paradise.

My point is, love is paradise—and Black love is paradise in a warm-weather locale. Stick it out if you can, Hill. It's sooo worth it!

Your Brotha,
Don

RESPONSE FROM ROBIN

Dear Hill:

I was raised to believe that Black people loving other Black people was a revolutionary act. You've met my folks, so that should not come as any surprise. I know that when we reach adulthood, we end up rejecting a lot of the ideas and beliefs we were raised with, but this is one that I actually came to feel stronger about. I believe it's true. I can see now, there's so much standing in the way of the success of Black couples these days, it takes real strength and courage to stand in the face of that, stay in a relationship, and make it work.

In our case, Don has probably already told you all about how we hooked up in college, but I'm suspicious of his version of events, especially because you probably heard it, like, more than twenty years ago, so God knows what he told you guys. Y'all were so hard on him when he decided to ask me to marry him. You acted like he'd said he was moving to the planet Pluto. Hey, is that even a planet anymore? I'd heard that it was demoted. But I digress. What I was saying is that I'm glad you asked me to answer that question because it gives me the chance to offer my take on things.

You asked what the biggest challenge is to a Black relationship. I'd have to say friendship. I don't think a lot of people find themselves in relationships with people they like and are friends with.

Think about the really good friends you have. You are able to talk to them, you trust them, you like them, and you want the best for them. That's how my parents describe their relationship. Even now, when they leave a restaurant, they hold hands as they walk back to the car. They're the best of friends. That's how Don and I are. It's always been easy for us to get past the difficult times because, when it comes right down to it,

> ❧
> **Be the best of friends.**
> ❧

we're friends. That's the part of our relationship we both miss the most when we're away from each other—the gossiping (he'll deny that he gossips!), the talks about current events and stuff the kids are into. And it cracks me up that he thinks he's some big ole Casanova with the ladies. You know the minute some woman really throws herself at him, he'll go running for dear life.

Some of my friends act like Don is the last of his breed, like they can't find smart, loyal, loving Black men out there. I don't believe it. I don't want to sound cliché or corny or anything, but Black men and women have always been pitted against each other. We've been made to believe so many lies about each other, and that's why I think our loving each other, whether it's expressed through friendship or marriage or both, is a revolutionary act. It means that we're able to see and accept the truth in each other, and in ourselves.

And in this world, what you see is what you get.

Okay, that's it, handsome. I hope it helps.

And when are you coming back to D.C.? My parents keep asking about you!

xo

Robin

When I read Don's response, the first thing I thought of was the Willie Lynch Speech. Is it true, as Don suggests, that in 2009 at the first sign of trouble Black men and women immediately run to fear-based stereotyped notions of each other? That we feed right into "he say / she say," "typical this . . . typical that" interaction? Robin's response offered that the cornerstone of their relationship is their friendship, which is the antithesis of the Willie Lynch goals of subjugating slaves and all Black people through self-division and mistrust.

Don and Robin *are* best friends. I've never once heard them gripe about each other in a "he say / she say" way. Their relationship is the type of love I want to experience. When love works well between two people, it is a simple thing of beauty, much like a well-tended garden. These are the relationships that seem stable and consistently loving. People who come into contact with couples in such relationships feel like they have been given the opportunity to bask in the glow of something special and extraordinary. Perhaps to have any hope of getting out of the rut of stereotyping and mistrust we will have to expose and examine what we say about each other. Let's explore our "he say / she say" habits.

3.

He Say / She Say: Who's to Blame

Men and women belong to different species, and communication between them is a science still in its infancy.

—Bill Cosby,
married to Camille Cosby since 1964

Perhaps the best way to begin a conversation of this magnitude is to clean the slate, stop the blame, and identify the poisonous roots. If I'm going to have any chance of getting past my own fears, I have to recognize the embedded stereotypes or negative views I hold. So I'm just gonna put it out there—some of the complaints I've heard from people I've met at readings and speaking engagements, from friends and colleagues, and a few from my own lips. These were the kinds of things that were probably going through my head as I sat there *not* calling Nichole because I was trying to figure out what she wanted out of our relationship. Of course, I had met her only once, so I didn't know what she was wanting or feeling, just what I thought a single mom ("typical") would want or feel. And we know what a great start that was. I'm acknowledging these stereotypes and views not because they are true or because they represent the amazing Black men and women I have met along my journey. Rather, I present these beliefs because they are perpetuated by so many of us, and they ultimately threaten our goal of achieving happy, long-lasting relationships. Most are sweeping generalizations that, over time, make us untrusting, vulnerable, scared, angry, frustrated, closed-minded, and negative. Is that any way to approach a relationship?

	Black Women Are Always Angry
HE SAY	"They seem to have a laundry list of unmet expectations. And it becomes a self-fulfilling prophecy."
	"I'm just tired of paying the price for all the men in her life who've hurt her, disappointed her, or left her high and dry."
	"It's like they are waiting for you to disappoint them."
	"I just want to be with a woman who knows how to have a good time without trippin' on every little thing."

Black Women Have an "I Don't Need a Man" Attitude

HE SAY

"They never let themselves be vulnerable enough to ask for help."

"Whenever we'd get into an argument, my ex-wife would tell me, 'I don't need your ass.'"

"Okay, so she makes more money than I do. A man still needs to feel like he is an integral part of a relationship, not some kind of financial burden."

"My girl would ask me to do something, and if I didn't jump on it at that moment she did it herself with an attitude."

Black Women Are Sexually Repressed

HE SAY

"She won't go down on me."

"My ex acted like making love was a chore . . . like she was doing me a favor."

"Once in the middle of passion I told her to bite my nipples and talk dirty, and she said, 'I'm not that kind of girl,' . . . and I said, 'What are you, a nun?'"

"My ex said to me once, 'If I did what you asked me to do you'd think that I was a ho.'"

Black Women Use Pregnancy to Trap Men

HE SAY

"My ex-girlfriend offered to go on the pill because we were monogamous, but I found out a few months later she'd never even started taking them."

"I love my son and I'm glad he's here, and I'm trying to be the best father I can be. I think his mother thought getting pregnant would guarantee that (1) I'd marry her and (2) having a baby would give her something that loved her unconditionally and would make her happy . . . she coulda gotten a puppy and we'd probably still be happy and together."

"My wife and I got married because she was pregnant. We have four kids now. Last year she confessed that she'd planned her first pregnancy without even telling me. I can't help feeling like our whole life together was based on a sneaky lie."

Black Women Let Themselves Go

HE SAY

"When we started dating, my wife wouldn't even let me see her unless she was wearing lipstick and heels. Now the only time I see her wearing makeup is when we're going to church or she's going out with her girls."

"The doctor told my wife that if she changed the things she ate and lost some weight, it would make a huge difference with her diabetes and high blood pressure. She won't do it. It's like she doesn't even care about herself."

"My girlfriend has cut her hair so short, she looks like a guy."

"When I met my wife she was hot and not afraid to dress provocatively, but now she dresses like an old school teacher."

Black Women Are Gold Diggers

HE SAY

"I was working in the mailroom at a law firm during grad school and I asked one of the junior lawyers out to lunch. She laughed right in my face. Loud, too."

"You can be the best man in the world; if you're not draped in designer labels or driving a fancy car, most of the women I know just aren't interested."

"The first question women always ask me is 'What do you do?' With a lot of women, when they hear I'm a surgeon, their faces light up and I can almost hear the *cha-ching* sound in their minds. Sometimes I tell them I'm a plumber, just to see how differently they react."

"When I got laid off, my girlfriend broke up with me, told me, 'I can do bad all by myself.'"

Black Women Always Travel in Packs

HE SAY

"I'm too old to wade through a group of women to ask one to dance."

"Women don't realize that they look like a human shield when they hang out in groups all the time. What brotha is going to approach all that energy?"

"I don't want to feel like I'm dating you and all your friends."

Black Men Are Lazy

SHE SAY

"They expect Black women to do it all—raise a family, work full-time, and do all the housework."

"My man's got two degrees, but he always seems to get jobs that pay about five cents an hour more than minimum wage. He's an underachiever."

"I dated this man who thought just showing up was enough, like Black women are so desperate for a man that they should settle for anything."

"By the time he wakes up I've already done twice as much as he'll do the whole day."

Black Men Are Playas

SHE SAY

"This man had me thinking he was a hot minute from marrying me; then I find out he's juggling three other women besides me."

"He looked me in the eye and told me he loved me. After we made love, he never called me again."

"After my boyfriend and I moved in together, he told me that I would always be his number one, but he still intended on seeing other women."

"After I dated a man for a year, he told me he was undecided and still needed to keep his options open. He said he 'loved' me, but he wasn't 'in love' with me."

When Black Men Become Successful They Don't Want to Date Black Women

SHE SAY

"It's almost like the White woman is a trophy, the prize for a Black man's success."

"I worked and supported our family so he could go to college and grad school. The second he got two cents to rub together, my ex-husband went and got himself an Asian woman."

"When I see a professional brother with a Black wife, it makes me respect him more because I know he loves and embraces every aspect of Blackness."

"How can these men look at their daughters and nieces and tell them that they're beautiful when it's obvious they don't really believe it based on the woman they've chosen as a life partner?"

Black Men Don't Take on Financial Responsibility

SHE SAY

"My son's father is more concerned about buying himself new toys and gadgets than paying child support."

"When we got married, my husband wanted me to pay half the rent like we were roommates or something; I said, 'No way.'"

"His credit was so bad that we couldn't buy a house together for years. Truth be told, mine wasn't that great either."

"I just feel like in addition to everything else, Black men expect the women they date to pick up their financial slack."

	Black Men Are Sexist and Misogynist
SHE SAY	"If I hear one more Black man referring to Black women as a 'ho' or a 'bitch,' I'm gonna scream."
	"Even if you have more education than them and make more money than them, Black men will still treat you like you're inferior to them."
	"How is it that so many Black men grew up fatherless and worship their mothers but have so little respect for Black women?"
	"I always had to pretend that I wasn't as smart or talented in order to make my boyfriend feel good about himself."

Do many of the comments above sound familiar to you? They certainly do to me. Notice how many of them come off as if there is already a built-in expectation of "that's just how it is between Black men and women." If we don't even like each other, how are we going to come together? To successfully transform the state of Black male-female relationships, I believe that we have to begin to fight against these types of thoughts and comments. These comments don't accurately describe *us*. They are fear-based comments: false evidence appearing real.

I saw myself in the rearview mirror that night in D.C. Maybe you know someone who has expressed similar frustrations about the opposite sex, or maybe you can identify with some of these thoughts yourself. Think about it. Be honest with yourself. Unless we are willing to have a conversation about all the things that are separating Black men and Black women, we will con-

> ❦
> Seal your lips against fear-based comments.
> ❦

tinue to stay stuck and be estranged from each other. The perpetuation of these types of generalizations absolutely affects the way we relate to each other.

You and I—*we*—have the ability to dictate how we relate to each other. We don't have to allow stereotypical notions or past experiences to immediately alter our personal future. We have to be mindful of what we reinforce by thought, word, and deed. We have the ability to change ourselves, those around us, and our communities *if* we decide to do it. But to do so first requires embracing how powerful each of us is. We all have the ability to be agents of change. The question is, are we willing to take the risk, open our hearts, and step out there to create new, uplifting relationships?

We can chart a completely new course simply by choosing to speak to and about each other in new ways. Let's commit to dragging the comments quoted above into the trash and pressing PERMANENT DELETE. Let's eliminate the poison and residual negativity that such comments yield. Nichole and I talked again, and we agreed that part of the problem was that we were talking to each other not like multifaceted people but like stand-ins for a cliché. It will take us collectively pulling up the roots of this kind of self-fulfilling teardown speech to create fundamental change. But let's not stop with discarding the "he say / she say" in our own relationships. Let's commit to two more actions that require even more courage. First, let's commit to publicly "checking," or stopping, someone from engaging in that kind of speech. I do this in the same way I check someone using the N-word in a certain way. Second, let's commit to referring to each other very publicly in honoring terms. "Hey, handsome," "How are you, Queen?," "What's up, King?," "Hello, beautiful." Words do matter. They matter in the negative *and* the positive.

Okay, so say we do these things. We're checking our negative stereotypes and preconceptions at the door. What are we going to replace them with? What *are* Black men like? If we bury the stereotypical notions that divide us, get rid of those things that we don't want, it opens the door to explore what we do want. What do Black men and Black women *really* want?

4.

What Brothers Want

—❦—

The biggest challenge would be communication. You just have to be able to compromise with your wife as far as I'm concerned. If she has a deep desire to do something, you may want to give in to that. My motto is, "Happy wife, happy life."

—Rev. Run,
married to Justine Jones since 1994

Okay, now, this is a subject I know a little somethin'-somethin' about: what men want. I know that more than a few of the sisters reading these words right now are probably saying under their breath, "Yeah, I know a little somethin'-somethin' about what men want, too: *sex*; that's what they want."

A lot of people, men and women, believe that to be true. But is it the whole truth? If it is true, then what does that mean? Does it mean that sex plays a role in the choice of a man's life partner? If so, how large a role does it play?

First things first: Is it true that all men want is sex? On the jacket of Dr. Louann Brizendine's recent book, *The Female Brain*, it is stated that "thoughts about sex enter a woman's brain once every couple of days [she didn't poll the women I know, lol] but enter a man's brain about once every minute." In her book, Dr. Brizendine goes on to explain that "males have double the brain space and processing power devoted to sex as females. Just as women have an eight-lane superhighway for processing emotion while men have a small country road, men have O'Hare Airport as a hub of processing thoughts about sex whereas women have the airfield nearby that lands small and private planes. That probably explains why 85 percent of twenty-to-thirty-year-old males think about sex every fifty-two seconds and women think about it once a day—or up to three or four times on their most fertile days."

I'm not in any position to dispute the good doctor's findings. Heck, I'll even admit to thinking about sex that often, if not more, when I was in my teens and twenties. However, I have known women in my lifetime who have had very healthy sexual appetites. And let us *not* forget that women have more nerve endings in their sexual organs than men and have the ability to enjoy sex more than men. Can you say multiple orgasms? So, yes, men do want sex. But I contend that it's not as high up on the list of wants and needs as many women—and even some men— would like to believe.

In his book *Act Like a Lady, Think Like a Man*, Steve Harvey very accurately lays out how simple we men really are. He writes, "Now men . . . are very simple creatures. It really doesn't take much to make us happy. In fact, there are only three things that every man needs—support, love, and 'THE COOKIE.'" In that regard, I want to explore something very important to men that many of us— especially Black men—have trouble admitting. We as men need to feel wanted in all ways. Our machismo often makes it seem like we don't care, but we do. Similarly, many women I know don't like to admit to needing a man or wanting to be protected by or provided for by a man, but many do want these things.

Simply put, men want to feel wanted, and I'm not talking about just sexually. While most women make their girlfriends feel wanted, they don't do the same with the men they date. I'm not talking about when a woman *tries* to make a man feel wanted, or simply acts like a damsel in distress. I'm talking about a woman's truly including a man in her decision-making process, asking him to weigh in on things that matter to her, and then valuing his answer.

One of my favorite songs by Prince is "If I Was Your Girl-friend." This might sound odd, but the lyrics are brilliant because they express in song exactly what I am talking about here. Do you have the capacity to treat your man as if he is your girlfriend? Not your girlfriend in a "gossipy" or "girly" way in terms of the level you include him in your life, but really making him feel wanted. One of the main frustrations I and many men have is when a woman is quicker to call her girlfriends or *mother* for "What should I do?" advice about something that's upset her (even if it's us) than to consult with her man (me).

What do I mean by that? I have noticed that one of the things my female friends do very well with their closest girl-friends is include them in their moments of success as well as their times of distress. They include them in talks about love, sex, and dating. They include them

> Inclusion makes your partner feel wanted and needed.

in their thoughts about their goals, dreams, and fears. The bedrock of that inclusion is that it makes the other person feel wanted and needed.

When a man marries a woman, his primary reason for making that commitment is not that he wants to have sex with her. Sure, sex is part of the agreement, the vow, but not the crux of it. I'm certain that sex is and was a significant component in the relationships of all the couples who were at the Blakes' anniversary celebration. But there is no way any of those relationships would have lasted five years, let alone fifty, if sex was *the* most significant component, or if that was all they had going. I have some happily married male friends who readily admit that the women they chose to marry were not as satisfying in bed as other women they had dated.

I think there are two reasons why a lot of people believe that sex is at the top of men's desires: (1) You can't walk past a newsstand without every female magazine screaming, "How to be better in bed so he'll love you," or "How to affair-proof your relationship with great sex," (2) Men are better able to compartmentalize than women. We can detach activity from emotion, especially when it comes to sex. For instance, a lot of young men have one-track minds. They're focused on their academic and professional goals, and they don't allow anything, especially romantic involvements, to distract them from their ambitions. But they still want to have sex. They are committed to sowing their oats and have no interest in a serious relationship. A lot of women aren't able to separate their emotions from their actions, especially when it comes to something as intimate as sex. This isn't an accusation; it's merely an observation. Neither perspective is more correct than the other.

Men are able to separate, to compartmentalize, and to view an activity through a narrowly defined lens. For a lot of men and some women, sex isn't something that leads to love and that promises or even suggests commitment. Sex is nothing more than sex, an enjoyable activity that takes place between two consenting adults. A lot of men say and do whatever they need to in order to have sex with a woman, and they don't see anything wrong with that. In the man's mind, it's recreational, nothing more and nothing less. Seemingly, what's important is for both men and women to recognize these different views and not judge each other. If both consenting adults know the other's expectations going in, there's no reason it can't be enjoyable and satisfying for all concerned. The problem comes when both parties aren't on the same page.

This brings us to the issue of readiness. I believe there is an interesting relationship-readiness paradox in our community. It seems that many more women believe that they're well prepared and ready for a relationship than they actually are, and there are many men who believe that they are not ready, even though they might be.

I bet you hear a lot of women—and men—talk about whether a man is ready to settle down, ready to get married. I know I do. That's all my male friends and I talked about—for weeks—when Don told us that he was going to propose to Robin. We didn't think he was ready. In our minds, there was no way he could be ready. We knew that because *we* weren't ready, and if we weren't ready, how could he be ready?

What exactly does it mean for a man to be ready? That answer differs from person to person, but it all boils down to feeling like you've become a man. For some men that means being the sort of man who can be the head of his household, who can take care of his wife and support whatever family he starts. That is the way I have thought about my "readiness" and where I think I have been mistaken. Rather than focusing on the idea of a partnership where we both can help each other achieve, I have always thought that I must be fully formed to be ready to go to that next step. For many men, being ready means that we've done our due diligence. We've gotten our education or training in the area where we want to achieve. We've worked the entry-level jobs that we had to take to pay for that education and formal training. We are able to take a date out to a restaurant that isn't part of a fast-food chain.

I, along with most of the men I know, was raised to prioritize career development. We were raised to first pursue our professional goals; personal goals came second. While we were pursuing those professional goals, there was no stigma attached to a man sowing his wild oats. In theory, he would get the desire to screw around out of his system before he got married.

That way of thinking is a difficult habit to break, and perhaps it's why some of my male friends have difficulty with monogamy. It's like encouraging someone to do something they enjoy, then reversing course and saying "You shouldn't enjoy all of that anymore; you really should enjoy this over here now." Or, like my grandfather used to say, "It's like giving a fat kid cake." It's easy to develop an appetite for it and it's not easy to go cold turkey off anything.

There is also a timing element for men. A few of my friends seemed as if they just woke up and said, "It's time for me to be married. . . . That's the next step in my manhood." Oddly enough, I have seen a man court one woman for years, and then six months later end up marrying the next woman he dated.

That is why, as difficult as it may be to accept, women should never take it personally; often, it is not about them.

Then there are men like my buddy Don, who met a woman and knew that she was the one he wanted to build a future with. Believe me, when a man finds himself in a situation like that, he will make himself ready, assuming he knows what he wants, not just what he thinks he should want, and his good judgment tells him that he'd be a fool to let an opportunity like the one he has pass him by. Men can be stupid, but we are not dumb. That's why the "he's just not into you" theorems are pretty accurate. Of course, I can't help looking back at my past with some regret over a few great women I let get away.

So what is it that men see in certain women that compels them to get ready? How did Don know he was ready? Honestly, I don't think those men want anything different from what other men want. I think it's just an issue of timing, that they were lucky enough to find the right woman early in their lives and were smart (and courageous) enough to act on it.

I have a lot of happily married male friends who say, "She makes me laugh. We have a lot of fun together. She's easy to be with. She's my best friend." They tend to smile a little when they talk about their wives. It's as if just thinking of them brings on a hint of joy.

Another thing I know is that men want to be with someone they can provide for, someone they can protect. That desire is just in us. Now, that needn't translate into a man needing to pay all of a woman's bills, or keeping her on a tight leash. It certainly doesn't mean that we're in-

> ✤
>
> They tend to smile when they talk about their wives.
>
> ✤

timidated by a strong, independent, successful woman. Providing for someone means being needed by that person. That need isn't always financial or physical. Providing for someone is also about offering emotional support. There are successful, powerful women who are married to men who don't have the bank account or high-profile job that they do. Many of these women say that their husbands make them feel taken care of. Take, for example, rising-star corporate lawyer Michelle Robinson (Obama) choosing to marry a law student without two pennies to rub together, whose only job was "working on a book."

To some men, being a provider means being the one who takes out the trash every night and fixes things around the house and assembles all the products and appliances that come in pieces and with instructions in a box.

Or it could mean being the one who picks up the kids from school or day care, arranges the play dates, cooks them dinner, and bathes them before bedtime. Roles differ from family to family, but the need to be a provider, to be counted on to provide a service of love—that doesn't change. The way I hear a lot of men tell it, it doesn't matter how much money a woman makes or what kind of job she has. It matters much more whether she is willing to create a space for him to occupy in her life, not in a nagging, demanding way but rather from an open and inviting perspective.

Most of the men I know are also looking for a woman who will make a good home with them, a woman who will raise their children well. That doesn't mean these men are turning over the entire burden of homemaking to their

> ❧
>
> There is nothing more appealing than a woman you can trust with your dreams.
>
> ❧

wives, but it does mean, they respect the value of a woman's touch.

A friend of mine, Mike, swears that all it takes is thirty seconds in a guy's home to realize that no woman lives there. "You walk in," he explains, "and the entertainment center is the most prominent thing in the living room. And besides maybe a dog, there's nothing else alive in that place except for him—no plants, no flowers." Mike's observations are long and pretty depressing, especially if you're a single man like me who can recognize elements of himself and his home in that checklist, but there's a lot of truth to what Mike says.

For my grandparents, making a home was a two-person job. There were things that my grandmother took charge of and things my grandfather took charge of. It's not so much about traditional roles as about each partner doing what he or she loves. I know some households in which the kitchen is the husband's domain: He cooks; she does the cleanup. Couples should define these roles however they want. It's no one else's business but theirs. The wife of a good friend of mine always insists on cooking dinner—in lingerie. He loves, loves, loves it, but never invites me over for dinner!

What about the issue of children? Fathers have a special relationship with their children. The absence of this relationship in a child's life is truly felt. The same is true of mothers and their children. If a man has decided that he wants to have children, then he will likely want a woman who not only wants to have children as well, but will be what the man envisions as a good mother to those children. Our definitions of good parenting are often based on what we either had or didn't have in our own lives.

Another thing that every man I know wants in a woman

is for her to believe in him and support his aspirations. There is nothing more appealing than a woman you can trust with your dreams, someone who will urge you to keep moving forward when you get tired, or when those dreams seem impossible to realize. And of course, men must support their wives in their own dreams, because they want to see the women they love happy and successful.

"Behind every good man is a woman"—but I like to think of it as "beside," not "behind." Many successful businessmen credit their wives as the unsung heroes of their success—and not because they ironed clothes or stayed at home and baked cookies. These women actually introduced ideas and policy. They made suggestions that turned into winning decisions.

Men want women who will help provide financial stability to their home life. There was a time when men used to turn over their entire paychecks to their wives, because men knew that their wives were responsible. Wives were the financial architects who made most of the monetary decisions for the household. In today's world of two-income households, many people oversee the management of their own individual funds. For truly effective partnering, however, there has to be some sort of communication and joining of funds to help grow familial wealth.

Men who are serious about having a real relationship want the following: a friendship and partnership that includes family; professional ambitions and successes; the creation and maintenance of a home; a solid and secure financial future; conversation; laughter; and, yes, *great* sex—lots of good, passionate lovemaking. I gather from my buddies' desires to

> ♣
> Beside every good
> man is a woman.
> ♣

call it a night early and get back home that it's the kind of love-making you keep thinking about until the next time you have your wife all to yourself and you're able to do it again.

I don't want you to take my word for everything—so I enlisted the opinions of a few of the regulars at my job, barbershop, church, and university to get their thoughts about what men want. Here is what some of them had to say:

BLACK MEN SPEAK I

Hill: All right, fellas. I have been getting bum-rushed by women across the country who all want to know one universal thing . . . What in the hell are Black men thinking? So let's go ahead and really break it down for them. I believe in the saying "Go hard or go home," so let's go ahead and jump right into it. What do women need to know, but not seem to know, about dating men?

Chris: That men are not as complex as women and so do not put the logical assumptions into play when it comes to rational thinking. Yeah, he was really watching the game and just did not think to call you and let you know it went into OT.

Brad: I think women need to understand that

a. You cannot rush a man into commitment. It will happen on his terms. If you try to force it, it will just create resentment on his end, and even if he gives in initially, the relationship won't work. You cannot forget that women outnumber men tremendously. Therefore, men can pick and choose who they want to be with. Also, a man is not sitting around thinking about a biological clock or planning out a wedding before he has a fiancée. Like it or not, all commitments are on the man's terms.

b. Being a man's friend is trusting him, listening to him, not trying to change him. . . . Let me say that again: *not trying to change him!* The man that you meet is the man he will be after years of a relationship. It is unfair to expect him to change because he has a woman now. At the same time, he doesn't want you to change either. Whoever you were when he pursued you, that's the woman he wants to be with later on. This means . . . stop having the representative work him over during the dating process and then showing up yourself only after the commitment. If you can't keep his interest by being your real self from the early stages, then he's not the one you want to be with anyway.

c. Find out what he likes—whether it be food, lingerie, poetry, whatever. I promise, if you do stuff he likes, he will do stuff you like.

d. Sex games are good. Play dress-up. Tease. Give him a lap dance and love his penis, and then if you are still unsure, please refer back to *a* through *c*.

Jared: Women need to know when to be quiet! I apologize for sounding like a jerk, but it's true!

Justin: Men like a woman who's confident. . . . Know your worth. If you know your worth, then at the very least, you will find a man who is worth what you are. It's not about how much money he has, how big his penis is, or all these other superficial things that women begin to want to build a marriage on.

Warren: You have to know who you are and what you want before you start a relationship. Look back at all of your experiences, and ask yourself questions like, What do I really like? What do I really need? What kind of man am I really looking for? Before you get into that next relationship. Because, from Tony down to James, if you keep making bad decisions without stopping to get to know yourself, you are going to start the same process all over again.

Khiran: I agree. Find out who you are and what you want. Until you do that, everything has been dictated to you by TV, popular culture, your mother, your girlfriends, comparing your man to their man, and their relationships—all these things. If you never take the opportunity to figure out what you want, then you will always continue in nonproductive patterns.

Darren: The core essence is all biblical. You really have to know who you are and your worth, and you have to be able to say, "Okay, I'm worth so much more than just casually dating this guy who holds some qualities but doesn't hold the qualities I know I'm going to need in a potential mate." It depends on where you are in your life, of course. If you're at that stage where you feel you are ready to be settled down and married, then you need to take that stance and not accept less than what you want. But if you are dating, having fun, and just enjoying things, then just accept that what you put into a relationship might not be returned or lasting. But you can still enjoy it.

Hill: When it comes to women, what are the ideal qualities and attributes that you look for?

Brad: My ideal woman is a confident, sassy, goal-oriented woman with a beautiful smile, nice legs, and pretty hands.

Eric: I look for a woman who is loving, trusting, trustworthy, forgiving, and fun. Physically, I prefer petite, shapely ladies with caramel or chocolate skin tones.

Jared: Before I got married, the top qualities I looked for were for her to be ambitious, moral, and supportive. As for the physical attributes, I love a nice rack and a pretty smile. My wife has all of the above. I am a happy, blessed man.

Hill: Congratulations; we should all be so blessed. My married brothas, and brothas who are in serious relationships, how do you feel you and your significant other have beaten the statistical odds?

Jared: We talk. Well . . . most of the time, she's talking and I'm listening. I think that our odds of success are much higher than the norm due to our long-standing friendship. We already knew everything about each other before we even decided to date. Friendship is key, and you can't forget to have fun with each other.

Chris: Well, being married at twenty-two and still together after fifteen years, I'd say that we are beating the odds, as more of our friends' marriages have failed than have not. But I think it is about not doing what is easy (leaving), and being committed to working it out, which is much more difficult, but ultimately worth it. We are building something together.

Hill: So what does a healthy, successful relationship actually look like to you?

Brad: Open communication, trust, true friendship, true friendship, and most important, true friendship.

Chris: One in which there is openness, trust, and forgiveness. You have to be able to communicate. When there are issues, you have to be able to talk or yell it out, but in the end, you have to be able to say "I am sorry" and/or "I forgive you." And be *true* to all of these, not just for the sake of keeping it together or to end the argument.

Jared: Longevity, mutual respect, and lots of sex!

Hill: What are the positives and negatives about being in a relationship?

Warren: It is the most beautiful thing to share life's moments with someone. The downside is that everyone is their own person and you have to take the good with the bad.

Jared: I love the fact that I can spend all the time with my wife that I want, and no one can make a fuss about it. It's like I combined a best friend and a lover and locked her in a lifetime contract.

Brad: The positives of a relationship include not having to conquer life alone, having a support system, a safe sex life, an extended family, financial security, and peace of mind. The negatives of a relationship are having someone to answer to, experiencing more problems and issues from extended family, feeling like you need your partner to maintain your lifestyle, and the pressure of keeping it going. Basically, the same reasons you love it are the same reasons you can hate it. You have to make the best of every situation in life. Love is no different.

Hill: Would you prefer to be single or attached?

Brad: I would prefer to be attached because of all the many positive things that come from being in a good relationship. Like companionship, shared experiences, being parents, great sex, celebrating victories, and on and on.

Jason: Most definitely attached. Being single has its advantages, but in the long run you are alone and that is not fun to me. There's nothing like coming home to someone, hopefully your best friend, every day.

Eric: It really depends on who you're dating. I've been in relationships where I'd rather be single. But if the relationship's good, then of course I'd prefer that.

Hill: It might surprise some women to realize that many single men would prefer to be in a long-term relationship. So with women wanting to be connected to men, and with men now saying that they actually prefer being connected to just one woman, why, then, do you think African American men and women are statistically struggling so much to have successful relationships?

Brad: I think the Black family has been shredded for a couple reasons. The last forty years have been filled with fatherless households and women struggling to take care of their children. As a young girl, if your mother (who probably resents your father for not being there) continuously tells you, "You don't need a man for anything. Provide for yourself! Take care of yourself. Look at me. . . . I'm doing it, and we are fine," at some point, that girl will begin to believe this. Then, that same young girl probably will not have the luxury of seeing her mom have a healthy relationship with a man. So, how is she supposed to know how to interact with men? On the flip side, in these same households, most young Black boys don't have male figures to teach them how to be men or how to treat women. What happens when this young girl and this young boy meet up when they are grown? Exactly what is going on now . . . you have two people who don't know how to deal with each other.

Chris: As men, we have been afraid to work as hard at relationships as we do at everything else.

Jared: Because as a whole, we're broke. Money always becomes a point of contention.

Kev: Check this out. I think it's because men ain't being men. Because men are not being raised by men. Once that started happening, women had to step up and come into their own. Take care of the kids and hold down the household. They are not supposed to have to do that on their own. If the man is not doing what he's supposed to be doing, everything falls down, and you have what we have today. That's why, for the past ten years, it's been this explosion of lesbianism. Now it's just everywhere. Because men ain't being men. Well, shoot, if I was a chick, and I'd tried dude after dude, shoot, I might have tried to turn to women, too! You know, we men, we are gruff; we ain't in touch with our emotions; some of us are unkempt, don't shave, don't always make sure we smell good; and we treat women wrong on top of that? If I was a woman, I wouldn't want that.

Hill: You mentioned the challenges sistahs may have with dating Black men. What are your challenges in dating Black women?

Brad: None at all, and I mean that. The challenges I have dating Black women are the same challenges I would have dating any woman. There are no challenges that are strictly specific to them, and I think that men who say so are using that as a cop-out excuse for their own shortcomings.

Chris: *None.*

Jared: Straight up, I think that many Black women are untrusting and insecure. It causes issues.

Hill: Do you all feel valued by Black women?

Brad: I think Black women appreciate what I bring to the table, as far as not being a statistic. I realize there is a shortage among Black men between jail, gangs, drugs, being uneducated, etcetera. So, being an educated, nonabusive, dedicated father with a strong family base and career has definitely increased my value within the community.

Jared: No. Black women have a negative view of Black men and rarely give us the benefit of the doubt. I hate having to prove myself over and over to Black women (professionally and personally)! I *absolutely hate* being interviewed for a job by a Black woman!

Dietrich: As a whole, I would almost venture to say no. I think Black women have taken an "I'm independent" stance and in many cases it isolates them. I even here mothers drill it into their young daughters, "Don't count on a man for anything . . ." But that's not necessarily their fault. We men have let them down, so they have turned away. It's *our* fault.

Hill: Is there anything else you feel that Black women need to know?

Kev: A good dude, who is really, truly interested in a woman, will not care about her "issues." They won't be a problem. When I would get involved with those women who did have trust issues, I would let them know, "Hey, it's okay. Keep not trusting me for as long as it takes you to see that I don't have anything to hide. I'm not trying to hurt you. My intentions are right." I know that sometimes only time will make them see what I have been all along. It's the men whose intentions are not right who will get frustrated with women's concerns and questions and then bounce in the end.

Khalil: Women need to stop confusing sex with love. It's lust. Don't try to make a situation more than what it is. If you take an honest look back at the relationships of all the people you have been involved with, and you take away the sex aspect, and instead merely focus on that person's qualities or their mind, I bet 98 percent of them would not have lasted a week without the physical portion. If you just had to deal with a person's mind, their personality, and who they really are, you would not have dealt with that person half as long, because sex clouds your judgment. Slow down and figure out what you are getting yourself into before you get physical so you can go into it with a clear understanding of whether what you have is lust or potential love for the long term.

5.

What Sisters Want

❦

It's very easy. He's so quick. And we respect each other. If I have any suggestions, he respects them. If he has any suggestions, I respect them. It's just, I don't know, easy. And fun.

—Beyoncé,
married to Jay-Z in 2008

Maybe you're doubting it right now, but I do believe I have some insight into women, though oftentimes in the face of my own fears I choose to ignore it. I have had the privilege of knowing many amazing women in my lifetime—as a grandson, a son, a nephew, a friend, and a lover. I couldn't help but learn.

Of course, every woman has unique goals, dreams, wants, and desires. From my experience, here's what I think women want: Women want to be heard. They want to be taken seriously. They want to be with someone who appreciates their intellect but still finds them sexy and desirable. They want a man who will be a good provider and not the kind of person who disappears at the first sign of trouble. As much as women want men who will take care of them in that "male" way, they also want someone who will warmly receive their caretaking. They want someone they can nurture, someone they can nurse through illnesses and loss and other forms of tragedy. Women want someone they can argue with, without feeling like they are being bullied or patronized, someone who might disagree with them but will not disrespect or disregard them. Women want a good man, someone they can not only have children with but also build a future with, a man they can depend on.

Both of my grandmothers found men who were good, and solid, and loyal. I know that these men were always sensitive to what their wives wanted or needed because I watched as they took serving dishes from their hands and said, "Honey, let me take that in for you." I saw how they got up early in the morning to rake leaves or shovel snow, mow the lawn or clean the garage, because they knew that their wives wanted the outside of the house to be as neat and aesthetically pleasing as they kept the inside.

So here's the thing: I have a good clue as to what women ultimately want. I've seen what it takes to be that kind of man. But somehow I forget it all whenever I meet a woman I am interested in and who might return my affections. I draw a complete blank, find myself trying to figure out what in the world she might want from me, and then worry that I might not make the cut.

In the many conversations I've had with women throughout my travels across the country, I have learned that most Black women love Black men. Some women shared how they feel that our strength is like no other. Many often also acknowledged our vulnerabilities. I was told that we are loved by Black women because of our wisdom, shared experience, and protective na-ture. One woman named Sarita was wonderfully direct and con-crete in her answer to why she loves Black men. She simply told me, "Hill, Black men are beautiful. They are strong. They are ca-pable. They are all that a man is supposed to be when they are re-alizing their innate potential. They are a true gift from God."

That statement touched me on so many levels. I mean, it was downright inspiring. But what was even more powerful and sobering was to learn the opposing side of these powerful emo-tions. So many Black women who do not feel equally valued and cherished by Black men. As one beautiful woman named Genell told me, "No, Hill, I don't feel valued by Black men in general. I think they give off this persona that they treat Black women like 'queens,' but I personally don't feel as appreciated as I think we should be. I feel Black men think it is our job to build them up and make them feel good about themselves, when they don't realize that we have to put up with just as much as they do!" Talk about being able to handle the truth.

I believe that this is where a lot of Black women are frus-trated. They seem to think that Black men do not want to take the time to understand them. Yeah, not exactly as inspiring as being described as "a true gift from God." This is why it is so im-portant that we begin to open the deep lines of communication with each other. If Black men never learn how Black women really feel, then we will have a much more difficult time giving them what they need from us. Nor will we, as men, be able to get to the space where we feel comfortable enough to be vulnerable and open up.

I've heard many women say, "I love Black men. I respect Black men. I desire Black men. But I feel like I am not getting the same in return. Am I wrong for feeling this way?"

I don't think we can ever be wrong for how we feel. We can only be honest in our feelings. It does not surprise me that Black women feel the way that they do. As men we are not socialized to share our innermost thoughts and emotions. Moreover, as Black men we have been taught to shield our emotions and to act as if nothing can get to us: muscular stance, tight jaw, a chain, and big rims—we are encouraged to embrace a "you can't f—— with me posture." So how can we figure out how to be open and vulnerable with the women we date? I don't have that answer, but perhaps it begins with us listening to and *really* attempting to understand our women.

Most women feel more comfortable communicating their thoughts and feelings than do men. This became abundantly clear when I was invited to an event called Single Sistahs' Soiree. This event allows women to come together for an evening of entertainment, good food, pampering, and mingling. It was the perfect opportunity for me to ask about the treatment and attention they receive from Black men. Here's what a few of them had to say:

SISTERS' SOIREE CHAT I

Hill: Honestly speaking, why do you ladies think you are single at this point in your lives?

Aishah: I haven't come across a man with the qualities I'm attracted to who is ready to be in a relationship.

Iyana: Honestly, I'm currently single because I chose a man that God did not choose for me, and it ended in divorce. So now I am developing my relationship with Christ and waiting for the one he has chosen for me.

Hill: What are some of your challenges in dating Black men?

Aishah: Just understanding their fears and generational ideals of what a relationship is and how to accurately communicate feelings.

Iyana: The first and biggest challenge I have when dating Black men is them coming up and introducing themselves to me. Seriously, they don't do it very often. After that, the challenge is getting them to be honest about what they want and expect from you, and lastly, them not taking it personally if you don't want what they want.

Sarita: I think for the most part, my challenges with Black men have been that the ones I have dated have been raised with a false sense of manhood. Their ideals and standards align more with BET and the latest "Big Pimpin'" hit song than with what my idea of a healthy relationship is. Of course, as I got older, I had to face that much of the onus for the challenges I was facing fell on me because of the patterns in the type of men I was choosing to deal with.

Hill: It's interesting. Many of you ladies seem to be able to also take responsibility for your past choices and actions, and seem to be willing to move on. What are your relationship hopes for the future?

Aishah: I hope to one day experience true unconditional love and to also have no fear of love.

Sarita: To live happily ever after with my Prince Charming, in a nice house, with a picket fence, two kids, and a dog. I am staying positive and actually starting to believe in the possibility of experiencing the fairy-tale American Dream. Hey, why not me?

Iyana: I hope for a relationship full of unconditional love on both sides, full of fun, one that's a great friendship that is complete with trust, honesty, and understanding . . . and intimacy that will blow my mind!

Hill: Do you feel valued by Black men? Why or why not?

Aishah: Yes and no—I feel that Black men know our worth, appreciate our struggle, and can relate to us better than men of any other race. But I also feel that Black men tend to take us for granted. I've seen many successful Black men toss us aside when we were the ones to uplift and bring them up.

Iyana: No, and I believe we as Black women have ourselves to blame. We are so "independent" and quick to tell a man that we don't need him, so he uses that philosophy for all women because he doesn't want his ego bruised anymore. I also feel that they don't value us because we don't require them to value us. We allow them to call us names, we allow them to praise shake dancers, and call girls, which makes them forget, or choose to forget, that we are very valuable to them.

Sarita: Not at all. Maybe because I grew up in Southern California, but Black men here do not seem to value Black women at all. They might value their mamas, or their blood sisters, but when it comes to having relationships, it has been very hurtful. I will say that when I have traveled to other states, especially in the

Midwest and the South, the Black men by and large seem to have a greater sense of culture and self, and therefore a deeper value for Black women. It shows in little things they do like opening the doors, being gentlemen, and just being kind to me as a Black woman in general whenever they see me out in public.

Brandi: Do Black women feel valued by Black men? That is a great question. I would say definitely not. You look at Asians, you look at Hispanics, you look at any other ethnic group, Jewish included, and they're taught to only date within their culture. An Asian girl, even if she doesn't date Asian guys, will never talk bad about them. An Asian dude will never talk bad about an Asian girl, or say negative things against her. But when it comes to Black women and men? A Black guy that's not dating a Black woman? They are usually quick to say, "I can't stand Black women." Or a Black woman who may be dating a White man? She will say, "I can't stand Black men." That's the first thing that comes out of our mouths. In any other culture, that's taboo. You don't do that. You were bred to not speak bad against your own culture. It's something that we have accepted amongst ourselves. I'm not saying it's our fault. I believe that it has to do with American society, going way back to slavery, and how they divided and conquered us. They split us up from each other, and I do think that's the root of it. Then after slavery, there came the social welfare system. The odds are like fifty percent of Black kids are born in poverty in comparison to like ten percent of White kids. What is a family to do, other than go to the government and say, "I need assistance," only to be told, "Well, you can't get assistance if you have a man in the house who is working." So, therefore, a mother who has five kids to feed, and a father who is working but does not make enough to provide for all the children, is forced to say, "You gotta go, so we can feed these children." As a result, you have these kids who are brought up on the welfare system, who didn't have their father, and three generations into it, they don't know that their great-grandfather wasn't there because he was told by the government that he couldn't be. They just think he didn't want to be there. So, this is what we have gone through to get to this point of devaluing each other.

Hill: Wow. Overwhelmingly, most of you said that you do not feel valued. Going a little deeper into what Brandi was sharing, why do you think Black men and women are statistically struggling so much to have successful relationships?

Genell: Because, Hill, I don't think anyone has shown us what a successful relationship looks like. Many Black men are raised thinking it's cool to be a player, and a lot of women think all men are dogs.

Aishah: Well, I've spent time analyzing this, and I think it is generational. I feel it goes back to slavery, when Black men had to separate from their families, from their wives and children. After things changed, we still struggled to maintain families, to communicate as a family, and to show each other love. That negative emotional dynamic has been passed down through the generations.

Iyana: Exactly. As a result, we don't know what a real relationship looks like. Even if we grew up in a household with both parents, we still never got the concept of relationship. We see images on TV and in books and call it truth. But what we really see is just two people who like each other, decide to have sex, and stay together. We never learned how to communicate and get to know someone. We never learned how to say no and not settle for something—anything. We want a relationship so bad that we will accept the first thing that we believe it is. We haven't learned how to forgive and properly heal in order to move past our hurts. So we end up infecting the next acquaintance with our hurts and begin a chain reaction. As a result, now we are back at settling and ignoring just so we can say that we are in a relationship. We have been taught that it's not okay to be alone, so we are convinced that a warm body will satisfy our loneliness, when often it creates more.

Sarita: I completely agree with everything everyone has said. Also, I think Blacks have become so educated and/or complacent that it is to our detriment in many ways. We think things that took place during slavery, or even during the sixties and seventies, are so far removed that they no longer impact our communities in tangible ways. By and large we refuse to accept or even acknowledge that our unique history in this country has directly led to our negative present-day conditions when it comes to our relationships and family structures. But the fact remains that our experiences have played a direct and devastating role in how we communicate, love, and value each other. Until individuals go within themselves to root out the damage that has been done, to the best of their personal abilities, it will be almost impossible to heal and move forward into productive loving relationships with one another.

Hill: I definitely agree with you about the responsibility for each individual to do some serious soul-searching before they jump into a relationship. Too many times we bring old hurts, old issues, old experiences, with us into new relationships. As a result, relationships that are trying to get off the ground and into the serious stage are not able to make it, because of what has happened to us in our past situations. That "baggage" is often never dealt with. And it comes back to ruin potential blessings in the present.

PART 2:
MR. AND MRS. BUTTA WORTH

FROM THE DESK OF HILL HARPER

9/8

- Me and my most ballin' friends seem to have tons of options, but my solid, less money-making friends don't get any love.

- My boys naively think I got it made. "All these beautiful women," they say...yeah, right. Hot body/beautiful face used to be all that was needed. I want something deeper...

- Nichole makes me smile.

Does she want me or does she just want a "man"?

6.

Will Mr. Right Please Stand Up?

————— ⚜ —————

I will throw my career away before I let it break up our marriage.
I made it clear to Will. I'd throw it away completely.

—Jada Pinkett Smith,
married to Will Smith since 1997

Hill, I'm telling you, man, ninety-five percent of the sisters out there are trying to date five percent of the men!" That is what my buddy Tyrone shouted to me over a beer, trying to compete with the music playing at our favorite sports bar. Ty went on to say, "You're lucky, Hill, because you're in that five percent, but a brotha like me, man . . . these sistahs make me work so hard. And at the end of the day, most of them aren't even serious about me."

Ty is one of the good guys—solid, level-headed. He never went to college but he's just as smart as many of the people with whom I graduated from Harvard. He works for UPS, owns a condo, and likes to travel. But virtually none of my girlfriends are even willing to give Tyrone a chance.

All things considered, I don't think most sisters are asking for anything unreasonable. So why is it that so many of them tell me that there aren't many good Black men out there?

There are a lot of decent, educated, hardworking, well-raised, single Black men out there. There are also a lot of Black men who haven't had opportunities at a formal education or stable family life. But they are determined and ambitious, ready to defy whatever odds society has placed before them. Once upon a time, men like that were called self-made. Some of society's wealthiest and most successful people proudly wear that label. But many of my female friends are unwilling to give a man like that a chance.

Now this might get me into trouble but I'm just going to write it. Many of my most jaded female friends want a man who has already "arrived" and there's nothing wrong with that. However, I've noticed that if many of these women hold up a mirror to themselves, they would realize that they are still "works in progress," as well. It is somewhat ironic that in certain ways they are so demanding of a potential mate. Surprisingly, these same women would not date men who have a similar job, the same bills, or even the same personality or general attitude that they themselves have.

Maybe it's because a lot of my girlfriends seem to end up falling for the image a man presents as opposed to the character that he possesses. Their desire to be with a certain type of man leads them to overlook the facts. My girlfriends aren't stupid or foolish, but even the most guarded, pragmatic people can force themselves to see what they choose to see, even if all the evidence is to the contrary. Take my friend Julia, for example. She's an expert on emotionally unavailable men. She's a tough lady, the vice president of a major bank. Now, Julia is not the kind of person you can just "get over on." When she was rising through the ranks, it was her ability to read and relate to people that made her stand out in that competitive environment. The customers loved her, as did her colleagues.

Still, with all her talent and intelligence, Julia somehow always seems to find herself entangled with men who are emotionally—sometimes even legally and morally—unavailable. She once believed a man when he told her it was his sister's voice on the outgoing answering machine, that she shouldn't leave a message because his sister would forget to tell him, and that because his sister was studying for her Ph.D., they could not have visitors at their place, which is why he always had to come to her place.

Then there was the man who spent two years assuring Julia that his marriage was over and that he'd be divorcing his wife "soon." Whenever Julia dared to question his sincerity, to wonder when "soon" really was, he would fabricate lies to keep her hanging on. He also made up with her by giving her gifts like Gucci purses or Prada shoes. She told me that all of the gifts didn't matter, but she never refused them.

I know one of the reasons Julia is so ready to believe is that she isn't truly open to being intimate. She says that she wants to be in love, but she keeps choosing men who can't give her what she needs. In her defense, things happened in her childhood that make it hard for Julia to trust men. So instead of dealing with her past issues, and because at her core, *she* is unavailable, she keeps picking unavailable men. By

> ❧
>
> Put down the magnifying glass and look in the mirror.
>
> ❧

choosing men who are not able to love her properly, she can focus on their relationship problems instead of looking at herself in the mirror. We have to put down the magnifying glass that we focus on others and look at ourselves and our own issues in the mirror. I think this is something we all need to do.

Now, Julia would probably argue with me about her having availability issues. But I know from my own experience that the fear of getting hurt or allowing someone so close that they risk reopening childhood wounds has hindered my own ability to be in relationships. I'm down here in the trenches with her because this is exactly what I want to work on with the help of this book. Let's look in the mirror, be honest with ourselves, and begin moving forward. It's time to get unstuck!

A lot of my girlfriends gush about how wonderful the men they've met are and how glad they are that these men "chose" them. I'm surprised because these friends of mine are smart, capable, talented, desirable women who play an active role in the choosing of everything else in their lives. When it comes to men, though, they seem to suddenly relinquish their power and become deaf, dumb, and blind.

> It's time to get unstuck!

There are times when I've had to say to a friend, "Really, you want to get involved with a man who has three children by three different women that he didn't commit to? What makes you so special that he's going to change in order to be with you?"

I've seen female friends of mine become so focused on what they want from a man that they forget their own accomplishments and value. Then they project onto the men they date characteristics that are more in line with their fantasy than with reality. After one date, some of my friends feel like they've found their soul mate and are so busy in that fantasy that they don't even ask whether the guy is right for them. They are planning their weddings and considering names for their unborn children as if they're still in high school. Rather than enjoying the process of meeting someone new, or truly getting to know their new man, they create a mythology without really knowing if the man is actually interested in a relationship with them. Imagine how intimidating that is for the guy! Men can smell the scent of desperation coming off a woman and can almost always sense when a women is more interested in having "a man" than having *them*.

This is not to say that dreaming is a bad thing or to imply that trusting is a mistake, but it's important that a man earn a woman's commitment and trust and that a woman really listen to and learn about a man with an open mind. As my grandmother used to say, "You can lose your heart, but keep your head." Women, trust your senses. Observe his *character*. As men, we are revealing our true character all the time.

> ❧
>
> You can lose your heart, but keep your head.
>
> ❧

A man I respect a great deal, Pastor A. R. Bernard of New York, says that "patience is a secret weapon that forces deception to reveal itself." If many of my female friends focused on a man's character first and foremost, they would end up wasting a lot less time with men who seem to fit the model they want but don't possess the character to build a real relationship with them. For example, the relationships I have taken most seriously are the ones that progressed from, as Pastor Bernard says it, *A* to *F* to *I*: acquaintance to friendship to intimacy. When we meet someone we are attracted to, most of us don't exercise the patience to explore the *F*; instead, we go straight from acquaintance to intimacy. That has happened too many times for me and that is why I am really trying to develop a friendship with Nichole before we get to the *I*. I am doing my best to resist my old patterns with her. I am going *A-F-I*—and it's not easy! But if I'm serious about wanting a new reality, I have to choose to act differently.

The wonderful thing about choice is that it gives us the power to take it or leave it. If a woman realizes that the partner she's chosen is not going to be what she wants in a man, or cannot provide what she wants out of life, she shouldn't be afraid to be alone. It's all right to just walk away. Too many women look at singleness as a death sentence, continue relationships they know they shouldn't stay in, and wait for the men to break up with them. But here's the paradox: We men don't like to break up with you either, so we begin to treat you so badly that you will be forced to break up with us. You end up with two people afraid of ending something that should of ended months or even years earlier.

> *It's all right to just walk away.*

My friend Julia takes this even further. She claims it's the reason why men step out on their wives and girlfriends and subconsciously do things to get caught—like taking a mistress to the wife's favorite restaurant or shopping for another woman at a store where everyone knows the wife. Julia thinks these men want to get caught and have the women end the relationship so they don't have to.

"How many times have you told a woman that it's over?" she asked me.

"I've ended relationships before," I told her.

"Directly? Did you sit the woman down and have a heart-to-heart conversation with her?"

I thought about it but couldn't remember a time when I'd done it quite that way.

"I knew it." Julia laughed, reading into my silence. "You probably stopped calling her, or kept seeing her but just kept growing more and more distant until she finally figured it out."

She was right. That exact scenario had happened to me in a past relationship, and I'm not proud that I didn't exercise the courage to just end it. It would have been better for her and for me. Instead we dragged our relationship through the mud. I would like to believe that I am a man of character, but I exhibited cowardice and she went with me. Whether we are conscious of it or not, we all are choosing the exact relationships we are having (or not having). As hard as it was for me to understand this, I now realize the truth in the saying: "There are no victims, only volunteers."

> ~
> There are no victims, only volunteers.
> ~

I was discussing this with my friend Janay, and she told me a story that really surprised me. I knew that she had been in a really positive relationship for the past two years, but she confided to me that if she hadn't met her boyfriend in the way she had, they wouldn't be together today. "He just wasn't my type—at all. . . . I almost blew it. In any other circumstance, I would never have given him the time of day," she said. However, they were seated next to each other on a cross-country plane flight. As she put it, "He had me as a captive audience. It took a while, but this man who I wouldn't even look twice at made me laugh and was wonderful to talk to. By the end of the flight, I gave him my number." How many people do all of us miss out on because at first blush they didn't appear to be what we think is "our type"?

7.

The Language of Men

❦

I'm glad I understand that while language is a gift,
listening is a responsibility.

Nikki Giovanni,
world-renowned poet, writer, commentator, activist, and educator,
and a mother since 1969

A lot of the women I've talked to ask me what's the best way to effectively communicate with a man. How can a woman know what a man is really thinking if she can't get him to talk?

It's almost a cliché to say that men and women communicate differently, but it does seem to be true. We're simply different. "It's like my boyfriend speaks a completely different language than I do," my friend Gail once said.

"That's because he's talking in the language of men," my other friend, Mary, replied. The three of us were having lunch.

"If you didn't grow up with it," Mary continued, "it may as well be gibberish." She explained that she hadn't grown up with any men in her house, and so she'd never really learned to understand the language of men—the sports talk, the sparse replies, the sudden and deep silences. She acknowledged that she had, on many occasions, interpreted her ex-boyfriend's silences as emotional cruelty. "I honestly thought he was just being mean, giving me the silent treatment. I'd ask him how he felt and he'd just give me a blank stare and shrug. It drove me crazy."

Both women then turned and stared at me as if I could magically reveal the tools to properly decode this language that men speak—if and when they speak at all. Unfortunately, all I could share were my observations.

Linguistics scholar Deborah Tannen considers male-female conversation a form of cross-cultural communication. The innate differences in how men and women think, act, listen, and therefore communicate are so profound that it is as if we are products of completely different cultures. These communication differences have been seen as early as the age of three.

I started this book by explaining how I believe that Black men and Black women don't really even talk to each other anymore. I grew up watching my grandparents sit and talk. They talked about everything—from the weather, to the news, to the neighbors, to the grandchildren, to their plans, and then back to the weather again. Watching those older couples at the Blakes' home reminded me of the flow and ease of my grandparents' conversations. I loved how the men joked with one another and with the women. I loved how the women were an integral part of the exchange, either adding something affirmative to their husbands' statements or putting forth an alternative view, not just talking among themselves.

I wondered why it seemed so special to see men *and* women gathered together and talking. Then I remembered a panel that I'd been a speaker on the previous year. It was an all-male relationship panel at the Essence Music Festival in New Orleans. I was intrigued (and, to be honest, scared) to be a part of it because I wasn't sure what was going to happen. I mean, traditionally, men are not considered big talkers—especially not when it comes to relationships.

The thesis of the panel seemed to be that through a combination of biology, brain chemistry, and socialization, men are "doers," while women are "feelers." When women talk, they feel comfortable expressing their emotions. From the outside, it seems to be a required part of their discussions. When men talk, however, it's usually about something specific—sports, business, home repairs, movies, television shows, or making money. We concern ourselves with the mechanics, not the emotions or the minutiae of these things. We focus mainly on the nuts and bolts.

That, obviously, is a generalization. The truth is that if you spend enough time in a barber shop, at the pool hall, on the basketball court, on the golf course, or at any bachelor party, sooner or later, golden nuggets of men's true thoughts, questions, and concerns about women and relationships will eventually come to the surface.

Even then, the revelation is seldom direct. It is often shrouded in humor or made to sound like a passing comment, not something to ponder, dissect, and comment on. If the other men do comment, those comments will invariably also be shrouded in humor or peppered with playful

> ❧
> Delivery is everything.
> ❧

insults and invectives—kind of like what happened when Don told us that he was going to propose to Robin.

When it comes to effectively communicating with men, how a woman says something is nearly as important as what she says. Delivery is everything. Here are three particular things I know men universally dislike:

NAGGING

Men definitely want a woman by their side who has their best interests at heart. However, there is a fine line between having someone's best interests at heart and aggressively forcing an agenda on someone. If a man has made it abundantly clear, in his actions if not with his words, that the topic you've decided is crucial enough to revisit countless times means nothing to him, give up. He is not ready to deal with it. He might not say that in so many words, but key in to his nonverbal clues. If he seems to shut down completely when you bring up a subject, then maybe you should back away a bit.

If it's something that you can't put off, try a different tactic. Draw him out by beginning the conversation with a question. For example, "How are you feeling about the recession? Is it having any effect on you? I'd love to hear how you're dealing with it." Nobody likes to feel as though they are being spoken at, rather than being spoken to, and a question makes it clear that you really want to hear his thoughts. Even if you respond with your own thoughts and you end up with a difference of opinion, at least you've both heard and listened to each other. Some women I've known deal with the fact that the men in their lives don't talk much by taking over the conversation. The only room the men are given to speak is at the end of the litany, and that doesn't seem at all like a space reserved for thoughtful opinion or an alternative view.

FISHING FOR COMPLIMENTS

You might just be looking for some reassurance and don't want to feel like you have to ask directly, but going fishing is a no-win situation for everyone. Let me give you a few examples of how this often plays out.

Scenario A

Woman: Babe, how do I look in this? Does it make me look like I've gained twenty pounds?

Man (hesitantly): No, hon. You look fine. You're as beautiful as you were the day I met you.

Woman: Is that supposed to be some sort of joke? I was thirty-five pounds heavier when I met you. I've been going to the gym every day, working my ass off to look good for you, and you don't even notice.

(Man drops his head and shakes it, suddenly losing all desire to go out to the dinner they'd been getting dressed to attend.)

Scenario B

Woman: Babe, how do I look in this? Does it make me look like I've gained twenty pounds?

Man (hesitantly): Don't get mad at me. You asked for the truth, so I'll tell you. It's not the most flattering dress you own. Why don't you wear the red dress you wore last—

Woman (upset):   I remember a time when you always used to tell me that I was beautiful, when you really appreciated me.

(Man drops his head and shakes it, suddenly losing all desire to go out to the dinner they'd been getting dressed to attend.)

No one wins in this situation. The woman wanted to hear that she is still the object of her man's affections. He thought she just wanted an answer to her question, and when he realizes that she didn't, the man feels like he was trapped. The more this sort of thing happens, the more frightened the man becomes about remarking on his woman's appearance at all, which means that the woman starts to feel the only way she can get a compliment is to fish for one, and the whole cycle just feeds on itself.

The solution to this problem is to be more direct about your feelings. If you're not feeling especially attractive or sexy, then express that to your partner. He might know just the right—and sincere—words to offer to make you know that you are loved. Also, when he does volunteer a compliment you appreciate, go ahead and tell him so, and let him know he's welcome to say things like that anytime he likes. With a little encouragement, most guys will figure out that if something works they should keep at it. We are, after all, very trainable, when we're given positive reinforcements and rewards. Just like a puppy.

DROPPING HINTS

Compliments aren't the only things women ask for indirectly. Unfortunately, men aren't always that good at picking up on those hints. If you want a guy to do something, be direct. Don't be coy about it. Just say what you want him to do. Obviously it shouldn't be delivered like an order or command in a game of Simon says, but I'm not the only man I know who responds well to the word *help*, as in, "Can you help me out next Monday? I've gotta put my car in the shop and I need someone to give me a ride to take care of a few things."

Everybody likes to hear *please* and *thank you*; nobody likes to feel taken for granted. Even if the two of you are married or engaged or have been dating for years and years, you can still ask directly and ask nicely— and show your gratitude when it's been done. (Guys, that goes for us, too.)

> ❧
> "Please" and "Thank you" are still magic words.
> ❧

I think sometimes women make too much of this so-called language of men. I believe that a man who wants to be an active partner in communication will be. If talking to your man feels like pulling teeth, maybe you should give your relationship a second look. See whether you've really developed a friendship. I know that men and women communicate in different ways, but we all share an understanding of what it means to be considerate of our partners.

Talking to someone you care about shouldn't seem like hard work. If it does, then maybe he is trying, through his silence, to tell you something. Yeah, I'll admit it; men can fall back on being passive-aggressive sometimes, too.

Withdrawal can occur when a man is overwhelmed by money, work, stress, or other things that he is trying to work out before communicating with you. So, it's not always a sign that a man is unhappy in the relationship when he turns inward. When something is bothering a woman, she usually doesn't hesitate to call a girlfriend to discuss her insecurities, issues, or problems. But that's not how the male brain works. Some guys just need to process on their own first. It's got to be an extremely serious problem for me to call one of my boys and say, "Man, I need your help. . . . I need to talk about something."

Denise, a married friend, doesn't agree, because her husband is a great communicator. He will pull her aside and inform her that he is distracted or feeling distant, explaining that it has nothing to do with her but with other things in his life that he is trying to process. She usually gives him a few days, but if he's still emotionally absent she'll jokingly attempt to pull him out of this "funk." Because he understands his wife and himself, he lets her know as soon as he recognizes this shift. Occasionally she'll be the first to confront him on his pulling away. The point is, they are able to have mature conversations about what's going on. She believes this is one of the key reasons she is still in love with her husband after all these years.

Of course, withdrawal *can* also signal that a man wants out of the relationship. As far as the woman knows, she and her man are still in a relationship, but in actuality he is long gone. The man resorts to silence, hoping that the woman will get fed up and make the decision to move on. That way he won't be blamed or held responsible for disappointing her, for shattering her hopes and dreams. It's difficult for a man to tell a woman he cares about that he doesn't love her anymore or that he does love her but not enough to remain in a relationship. At times, cowardly men just remain silent, and as I said before, I was one of those men.

Unfortunately, people respond to uncomfortable situations in a way of their choosing, not ours. Just as we intuitively know when someone is into us, we also intuitively know when someone is not into us. If you're willing to discuss the situation in order to stay together, but your partner is not interested in even talking about it, that alone should tell you where he (or she) stands. No amount of rationalization or excuse making is going to change what you already know deep down is true.

I'm not trying to place the burden of truth on the women's shoulders. This book is about relationships, starting the conversation that all men and women need to have and maintain in order to survive the odds and overcome the obstacles. If you're with someone who refuses to talk, the conversation is over. Period. It's as simple as that.

The distance that was present when I finally reached out to Nichole was created because I hadn't honored our initial connection. During that first call, it was obvious that she was guarded, not as open and forthcoming as she'd been the evening we'd met. And that's understandable. It was awkward, our conversation full of odd pauses and nervous chuckles. I ended the conversation by telling her, "I'll call you tomorrow."

It took a whole lot of strength, though, for me to call her a second time. I wanted the connection to come easily again, as it had when we met. But I knew that I'd have to work for it. I'd have to earn her trust, let her know that I was serious about getting to know her. I'd so admired the vulnerability Nichole displayed when she'd asked, "Will you call?"

I realized I had to allow myself to be vulnerable, too. Nichole had to be able to detect in me the same sincere vulnerability that I'd detected in her. Had I not been ready to grow, I would have resorted to rationalizations. I would have convinced myself that I'd done nothing wrong—*After all*, I would have told myself, *I'd promised her that I'd call, and I did call; I never said when.*

In fact, I almost started down that road. But when I did, I'd catch myself and ask out loud, as I had that night, "Who do you think you're fooling?" So I called Nichole that second time and I started the conversation by doing something I should have done during the first phone call; I apologized for letting so much time pass between the night we met and my call.

"I enjoy talking to you," I said, "and I look forward to getting to know you better." It wasn't a line; it was the truth—and that's what made it so difficult to say. I felt exposed. I ended each of those first few conversations by telling her when I'd call her again. And each time, I kept my word—because if people don't respect your time, it's an indication that they don't respect you. I wanted to lay a solid foundation for a possible relationship with Nichole. Eventually that easy, natural connection Nichole and I had returned, and our phone calls fell into their own natural rhythm.

While we're on the topic of communication, I want to bring up technology. In this new, cool world of high-tech, low-touch communication, we have the ability to send messages to anyone, at any hour, using any one of a variety of media. Whether it's Twitter or Facebook or e-mail or voice mail, we have no shortage of ways to talk. But are all these new advancements helping or hurting our communication?

There was a time when the only way to interact with the object of your affection was by being in the same room with him or her. When lovers were out of visiting range, they had to write letters. Now technology has changed the game completely.

When I have to quickly let a friend know that I am running late, I wonder how we ever got along before cell phones. Even if I know the person I'm trying to reach can't answer his or her phone, I can send a text.

The same technology that helps us to communicate can also hurt the quality of that communication, especially in romantic relationships. Many men don't like to have confrontations with the women they're dating. Is it any wonder, then, that so many of my female friends tell me that it is becoming more and more common for men to use text messaging to back out of a date with them, or even to break up with them? With text messages you can get your point across without any lengthy or uncomfortable explanations. It's also easier to manipulate the truth. Many of my male friends write things in text messages that they would never have the courage to say if they were looking the woman in the eye. And what's worse, many of my female friends allow men to get away with this type of "conversation."

We can also use the technology as a diversion. For instance, I am not proud to admit that I have sent the text "What are you up to?" to someone I was dating when I knew I didn't want to talk to her for the rest of the day but I wanted her to think I was checking on her. Not good.

Even if couples use technology to manage time and find ways to be more effective and efficient, it is still important to be aware of the ways in which we communicate with each other. Unless we're careful, relationships have the tendency to resemble business negotiations: We're dealing with our individual schedules, our kids' schedules, family dramas, financial decisions, social obligations, work and/or school commitments, professional deadlines. Those details can be all-consuming, and before we know it, all that other stuff has taken over the relationship.

> ❧
> Nurture true and consistent personal connection.
> ❧

Modern technology can expedite working out all of those details, but it can also make us feel as though we've had our fill of communicating with our significant other. By the time you two are actually face-to-face, in the same space, you're all talked out, even though you haven't really *said* anything. Before you know it, a relationship can be absent of any true and consistent personal connection.

You might think that sounds extreme, but it's very possible. I'd even say it's common. These high-tech methods of communication can sometimes cause a lot of confusion in relationships. There is no eye contact; there is no body language; there are no facial expressions. The nuances that come from tone and voice, and the visual cues we use to understand the significance of whatever is being said in person, are completely lost.

If you're face-to-face when a misunderstanding begins, you have the ability to say "Stop! That's not what I meant," and to correct whatever has been misunderstood. In person, we have a real-time awareness of when things are going right and when things are going wrong. The problem with "flat" mediums like texting, e-mailing, and instant messaging is that sarcasm sounds mean and jokes may sound dismissive when you don't have the intonation that makes them make sense. Statements meant as hints can sound like nagging or have no force at all. There are just too many ways for it to all go very, very wrong, very, very quickly.

I'm not saying that if a person e-mails or texts *I love you* to his or her partner, the person doesn't mean it. Plenty of couples find inventive and positive ways to use technology to enhance their personal communication and, thus, their relationship. But relationships are made in person. Communication is strengthened by looking into a partner's eyes, by holding hands while conversing, and by having the courage to say what's going on in our hearts, minds, and souls.

Just as we need to step up with our actions, we need to speak up with our emotions. We can't hide behind the ease of technology, the excuse of gender tendencies, or the history of our own bad habits. If we want to be with someone, we need to learn how to communicate—how to have our say, how to let someone else have his or her say, and, most important, how to find common ground.

8.

Checking Baggage: *The Lightness of Being*

───────── ❧ ─────────

Almost everyone today who has experienced a failed relationship is carrying around some degree of emotional baggage. The problem with these leftover feelings is that they are usually negative in nature, causing fears and doubts that carry over into future relationships. It's time for all of us to recognize our baggage and check it—in order for us to succeed in our relationships.

Eva Kingsford,
a single freelance writer some depict as a Northern star turned
Southern belle living in today's world with yesterday's ideals

I'm subtitling this chapter "The Lightness of Being" in reference to the novel *The Unbearable Lightness of Being* by Milan Kundera. The novel's central character, Tomas, is a womanizer living in Prague in the late 1960s. Kundera uses Tomas's journey to meditate on lightness and heaviness as states of being, or ways that we approach and experience our lives. I want to use his term as a means of broaching a sensitive topic.

Let me start with a story:

My friend Cheryl has a best girlfriend, Jasmine, who has been single for a number of years. Being a good friend, Cheryl would like to see Jasmine in a happy relationship, and so she asked me to set Jasmine up with my friends. I hadn't met her, so I asked Cheryl to describe her friend. "Jasmine is great," Cheryl told me, "so much fun. She's a great conversationalist, funny, full of energy, and she loves to have a good time."

I figured, cool. I saw her picture: she was cute; plus she had a great job, and even her name sounded fun . . . Jasmine. Cheryl is a good judge of character, so I happily agreed to set her up with a few potential dates.

After Jasmine had gone out with some of my friends, I asked how the dates went. The response was a shock. "Oh, Hill," they all said, practically moaning. "She was so boring. So serious. A stick-in-the-mud. She brought me down. I thought she was my grandmother." I was confused. This wasn't the friend Cheryl had described to me, and I couldn't imagine Cheryl hanging out with someone who was as down as the woman who showed up to meet my friends.

So I talked to Cheryl and told her the story that one of my friends had told me. He had taken Jasmine to a nice restaurant and—wanting to get her to loosen up a little bit—he ordered a great dinner with a really nice wine pairing. When the waiter put the bottle on the table, Jasmine looked up at my friend and said matter-of-factly, "Oh, I don't drink."

>   Joy spreads.

When I got to this point in the story, Cheryl literally gasped. "What? She and I were doing Patrón shots last week."

When Jasmine is with her girlfriends, she clearly has a certain "lightness of being." She's happy and relaxed, and her joy spreads to everyone around her. What man wouldn't want to date that person? But for whatever reason, when she's out with a man, all of that shuts down. All of that energy and "lightness" is replaced by a dour, "heavy" substitute. Anyone who's been hurt by someone close to them has reasons to be cautious in a new relationship, but Jasmine wasn't even showing up. She anticipated disappointment, and it became a self-fulfilling prophecy. The relationship was killed before it even had a chance to begin.

I have a number of female friends who tell me that they can't find a man, that they can't even get a date. When they finally do meet men, though, they seem disinterested. I have another group of female friends who tell me just the opposite. Their phones ring off the hook, and they are never without a date when they want one. Their lives are filled with men who want to take them out and treat them well. They have a surplus of men who want to be their friends, men who want to be their lovers, and men who want to marry them. In fact, a few of these women have gotten married in the past couple of years.

Jasmine's experience made me wonder whether that aspect of "lightness" made the difference. After all, one group was not particularly better-looking than the other. Neither group was more successful, or more famous, or even wealthier. The main element that differentiated one group of women from the other was their *presence*, with some of them embodying the kind of internal quality that men are just drawn to.

Most of my male friends, when they look for a partner, respond intuitively to that "lightness of being"—and I am certainly not talking about skin color. I'm talking about something that exists below the surface.

In the "I can't find a man" group, I noticed how much heaviness and seriousness the women carried. It is a mood that precedes these women into every room they enter and hangs over their heads like a dark cloud. The women in the other group have an attitude of joy and an ease of being surrounding them.

The lightness that I'm referring to isn't a lack of seriousness. These women are taken very seriously by those in their personal and professional circles. They are literate, focused, and conscious and serious about their lives. And sure, they have their days when they're feeling down. But they are not carrying a chip on their shoulders. Their baggage isn't weighing them down. They aren't defensive. They aren't afraid to open up to a man they're seeing the way they would to one of their girlfriends and let him help her feel better.

The distinction is one of perspective. It's about being the sort of person who sees the glass as half empty or being the sort who sees it as half full. It's about whether you're an optimist or a pessimist, whether you forecast failure and disappointment or expect cloudless skies and success. The lighter women seem to embrace a certain curiosity. Their energy constantly moves outward to engage the world, and what they bring is lightness and positivity. They are open and eager to engage. The effect this has on other people is one of attraction. People are drawn to them. Why? Because joy is contagious, and people are hoping to catch a little bit of it.

> ❧
> **Embrace curiosity.**
> ❧

The irony is that on "Girls' Night," many of my girlfriends are the life of the party. There are big smiles all around, and they exude true comfort and joy. But for some reason, this joy often disappears when men enter the equation. I have even experienced this with my ex. One day I walked into her place while she was on the phone with her best girlfriend. She was talking loud, laughing, and having an extremely fun and energized conversation. When she hung up, she turned to me and with almost a blank face said, "Hi. How was your day?" I wanted to say, "What happened to the girl who was just on the phone? I want to date her. . . ." But clearly, we had fallen into a pattern of heaviness with each other.

Brothers also have their own version of this heaviness. Our ego-based needs to "look cool" or "be hard" can lead us away from our true animated and fun selves. It's what I call the "Shaq media-training syndrome."

A number of years ago, I did a movie for kids with Shaquille O'Neal. I discovered he was this clever, amazingly dynamic prankster with a huge, generous spirit. We had a great time on the set. Later that year, I saw him being interviewed after a play-off game. I was so surprised by the person on the screen. He answered all the questions almost stone-faced. He looked super-serious and had no animation or energy, giving monosyllabic answers like "I—shot—the—ball." The Shaq I did the movie with was funny, vocally animated, and a joy to be around, but that's not the guy who was being interviewed. I could only think someone or some bad experience must have taught him to not be himself during postgame interviews.

We all can put on masks of heaviness to protect ourselves, but if we have allowed our baggage or someone else's faulty training to make us heavy, then it is up to us to rediscover our lightness of being with each other. When's the last time you said, "I got three jokes for you. Here they are . . ."? When's the last time you went out and did shots with a date? When's the last time you were on a date and you said "Forget dinner; forget the movie; let's drive up to Lover's Point, raise our hands, and scream at the top of our lungs, 'I'm the king of the world!'"

My friend Mary joined a popular online dating service. "It

was one of the best things I could ever do for myself," she told me. "Here I was, going on and on about how I wanted to be in a relationship, and I realized while I was putting my profile together that if I were a man, I wouldn't date me. I had lost my spontaneity and ability to really enjoy my life. I had to get that back—not for some man; for myself."

What I would say to all my sisters (and brothers) like Mary who might find that they are on the heavier side is this: To find your way to lightness, you must know that joy matters. Right here, right now, you might be having a very difficult life. Lots of people are. But some people manage to find happiness no matter how bad the situation is. I believe we can choose to follow that path, to exist in that way.

> Find spontaneity.

People who have lightness about them are having fun. They inspire other people to have fun as well. They laugh easily. They are comfortable in their own skins. They don't have the time to sit around and sulk over not being able to meet people, because they are having too much fun to care. In life, you shouldn't have to pursue what you can attract.

We all want to be near the "shining" people. Look at little kids: When they see somebody with lots of charisma or joy, they want to go stand near the person and share the joy. The truth is, we all want to share the joy, but as we get older, we become self-conscious about walking over and standing near a stranger simply because he or she shines. To me, women with that lightness are the most desirable women in the

> Share joy. Claim happiness.

world because it means that they've found a way to keep their lives balanced and to still embrace the very best that life has to offer. They are doing more than existing: They're living. They're doing more than hoping for happiness: They are going out and claiming it. What man wouldn't want a woman like that?

9.

Status vs. Potential: *Looking at the Obamas*

───────── ❧ ─────────

The most common ego identifications have to do with possessions, the work
you do, social status and recognition, knowledge and education, physical
appearance, special abilities, relationships, personal and family history, belief
systems, and often political, nationalistic, racial, religious, and other collective
identifications. None of these is you.

Eckhart Tolle,
spiritual teacher and author who has shared a long-
term partnership with Kim Eng since 2000

One of the things I've heard a lot from young brothers and
sisters during my recent travels is "I want a woman like
Michelle" or "Why can't I meet a together brother like Barack?"
In truth, they might be that person every day. These young
people are seeing the finished product, the result of years and
years of work and struggle. A few years ago, all Barack Obama
had was potential. I jokingly remind sisters that when Michelle
met Barack, the car he was driving around in had a hole in the

floor of the passenger's side so big that you could see the street. I ask the brothers whether they would be able to handle being with a woman who was their boss, because that is what Michelle was to Barack when he worked that summer at her law firm.

People tend to look for status in a mate when they should be looking for potential. What is status? It's pretty much the same thing whether you're in a relationship or not. It's authority; it's money; it's nice clothes and a fancy car; it's a good job. Status is swagger. And it's appealing to a lot of women.

But that type of status can be superficial and fleeting. Jobs come and go. Money also comes and goes. Without the window dressing, it turns out that some men are completely deflated. It's what makes them—and it's also what breaks them.

On the flip side, for men, status in a woman is often her beauty and her body. A woman with a good job, a fancy car, nice clothes, her own money, and some authority can be intimidating to some men. That type of man isn't sure why she would need him. If she's the boss at work, that might very well mean that she'll expect to be the boss in their relationship, and when it comes to status, some men don't like to share.

Physical beauty has been proven time and time again to be superficial and fleeting. Those of us who've been to our ten- and twenty-year high school reunions can attest to that. After two decades of life's hardships and disappointments, you might not even be able to recognize the woman who was the most beautiful girl in high school or the man every girl would have killed to have just one dance with.

Even so, we often find ourselves going for those very things— the superficial and fleeting forms of status. Then we wonder why the man who seemed so powerful and impressive in his three-piece suit doesn't seem so sexy after he loses his job. When the woman who'd had the power to make our hearts flutter and heads spin gains thirty pounds after a prolonged illness, we suddenly lose interest in getting her number.

I tell young people that instead of settling for status they should be looking for potential, and that means looking beyond the external. After President Obama graduated from Harvard Law School, do you know what he did? He spent the next year writing a book. That's right. He didn't go for the big-bucks job at a corporate law firm. When he did start working more formally, it was as a part-time constitutional law professor and part-time civil rights attorney. I'm pretty sure you're well aware that they don't make nearly as much money as full-time corporate lawyers do. Without an awareness of his potential, his wife might have thought he was an underachiever. She was the primary breadwinner in the household for the first several years of their marriage. He'd worked for next to nothing as a community organizer; he'd interned at a law firm but then hadn't gone on to practice law full-time; and then he wanted to continue in public service, still earning very little money. In 2003 he was soundly defeated in a race for Congress. All the while, our First Lady continued to be the primary money earner in the family. Early on, did Michelle's girlfriends say, "Girl, you could do better?" I don't know; I've never asked. Did she say that to herself? No, she didn't.

Potential is an individual's capacity to grow, to get, and to go the distance chasing his or her dreams. You might meet a man who is broke because he's working a full-time job that does not pay a lot but will benefit him in some other way. It's important to see

❧

Honor potential.

❧

past the limited cash flow to the things that he can, and likely will, achieve in the future. That's the journey you sign on for.

But the onus is not all on women to look for potential. When a man dates beautiful women who are interested only in makeup, designer fashion, and fancy cars, he is usually not looking at their potential. The woman who has the potential to help him reach his goals is most likely the sister who is together and focused enough to have finished school and gotten an enviable career, or who's working toward one. The fact that she can buy her own designer clothes and purses means a man's ability to do so is less of a priority for her when she's dating; she's interested in who a man is, not in what he can do for her. Rather than feeling intimidated by such a woman, men should feel inspired by the fact that she's a woman who is able to stand on her own two feet.

Status seeking happens in other contexts as well. Just the other day, two women were in my office for a meeting. I see each of these women often, but they had not seen each other in well over a year. While we were getting organized before we got down to business, the women used the extra time to catch up with each other. The first one, Jackie, asked the second, Renee, how she was doing. In response, Renee, who is newly married, held up her left hand to show off her wedding band and the immense rock on her ring finger.

"Oh, I'm doing *fine!*" Renee replied. After a slight pause, Jackie said, "Congratulations," but I could tell that there was a twinge of one-upping going on. It seemed just like the way a man brags that his car or rims are nicer than someone else's. Not to be crude, but I felt like I'd just witnessed a female "pissing contest."

This exchange was fascinating to me. I've seen, in my own life and among my male friends who are in relationships, the sort of pressure some women feel to get married. Watching this interaction between Jackie and Renee made me wonder whether in some instances marriage exists as a social convention that is bigger than the actual relationship between the two people who are in involved.

When Renee held up her hand to show off that huge rock, she wasn't saying "I'm in love." She wasn't gushing about how she had found a wonderful man, about how he loves her more than anything and makes her feel like she is the most special woman on earth. All of that could be true, but her action was saying, "I did it! I got *the ring*." Her message had more to do with status than with emotion.

I suppose that's what used to make me retreat into myself in the way that made my friend Julia refer to me as "emotionally unavailable." I was stuck wondering what the woman I was see-ing wanted from me and from our relationship. Did she want to be married to me, or did she just want to be married?

If our goal is to be with someone who truly cares for us and has our best interests at heart, then we need to take a true look at intentions, both theirs and ours. One of my best friends recently went through a difficult divorce, and she confided in me that when she married her husband, she didn't do so because she thought he was right for her. She did it because she felt pres-sure from her family and friends to be married, right away. I am a romantic and I want to be married. But when I do marry, I want my wife to know it's happening because of her and all that she is, and nothing else.

Years ago, my friend Carla told me that the best date she'd ever had in her life was when a grad student invited her to dinner. He was in his late thirties and clearly didn't have any money. He'd apparently had a career but decided it wasn't fulfilling and went back to school to obtain a degree.

Carla said that most of the men she was dating would take

her out to elegant restaurants. Then the two of them would sit there through three courses, sipping expensive wine, spending the whole time trying to break the ice. This man showed up at her place holding a big ole basket-looking suitcase in his hand. After she'd invited him in, he set it on her coffee table and opened it. He pulled out a blanket and spread it on the floor of her living room. Then he started pulling out plates and wineglasses, until her living room was picnic ready.

He'd prepared tuna sandwiches and a salad, with potato chips on the side. For the wine, he'd brought a couple of bottles of Trader Joe's "Two Buck Chuck." He'd brought a box of Girl Scout cookies for dessert. He'd even thought to pack candles and music. Carla thought it was the most thoughtful and considerate gesture anyone had made to her in a long while.

"Most guys would just choose a restaurant, make a reservation, and take you there," she said. "But this guy actually had to spend time thinking all this through, getting it ready. It was incredible. It didn't bother me at all that I was eating a tuna fish sandwich on the floor of my living room with him."

If Carla had been interested in status, what would have mattered to her was what restaurant she was being taken to. She would have cared what the Zagat rating was, whether the restaurant was popular, and whether the man would impress her friends and family. But because she was looking for potential, what truly mattered to her was not the food or what anyone else thought about her date. She cared about the time and effort and attention to detail that was put into the experience this man had created for her. They dated for a year, and then after finishing school, he found a job in another town and relocated. When I asked her what he was doing now, she told me, "He's at the top of his field. I read about him all the time in the papers. He's married with a son."

The very fact that so many years later Carla still remembers this guy and that first date, and still talks about it as the best date she's ever had, says a whole lot. I understand where she's coming from because I had my own similar situation. I dated a lady in my mid-twenties who would leave me little notes with messages on them. I'd sometimes find them in my car or in my pants pocket; once I found one stuck in the pages of a script that I was reading for an audition. These notes would often have little messages on them, like *Practice Love, You Are Amazing, Smell a Flower Today,* or *Shine!* Sometimes they were written as coupons: *This entitles you to one kiss and lunch at a place of your choosing.*

I was completely moved by the time that it took her to write and to hide these notes. It was time that she'd spend thinking of me and how to make me smile. Our relationship lasted two years (I screwed it up because I was young and I didn't realize what I had) and I've never forgotten those amazing notes and I have always remembered her with great fondness.

> True power lies in one's ability to create.

These are the sorts of activities that help people understand where true power lies. True power lies in our ability to create, to make something out of nothing, to invent a way where there was no way, and to build what others had only envisioned. That ability is potential, and it's worth waiting for. Based on what I've seen, I can't imagine anything more wonderful for a couple than helping and watching each other reach their *true* potential.

PART 3:
TRYING *Not* TO SLEEP IN THE BED YOU MADE

FROM THE DESK OF HILL HARPER

11/15

- The sex is good, but that's not enough to keep a relationship together. I made the mistake of thinking that before.

- I'm conflicted - a strong partnership is something I want, but I'm not really sure I want to deal with all the hurdles that come along with getting it.

- Nichole wants me to be just with her. Why is it so hard to break things off with other women?

- She compliments me.

> What if I choose the wrong one? I'm afraid I'll be stuck.

Am I gonna screw this one up, too? Why can't I COMMIT???

10.

Commit-Men-t

—⚜—

Wise commitments do not bind us; they free us. To the spiritually immature, "commitment" is a very scary word because it is internalized as bondage. But to the spiritually mature, commitment is the equivalent of freedom because it bestows authentic happiness that cannot be taken away.

—Rev. Michael Bernard Beckwith,
married to Rickie Byars Beckwith since 2000

*C*ommitment is a word that scares a whole lot of people. I'll admit that until recently, it scared me as well. The only reason it doesn't now is that I've figured out a way to make it not seem so overwhelming. I'll share that with you in a bit, but first, I want to take a look at why that word, *commitment,* is so scary to so many of us. One of the many definitions of commitment is "a pledge or promise." Not so bad, huh?—especially if you're a person of your word. If you make a promise to someone, then you should keep it. You would want to keep it. After all, you're the one who made the promise, right?

But that's not usually the first thought that people have when they think of commitment. Sometimes they think of another definition of the word: "consignment, as to prison." For a lot of people, commitment feels like a trap, something that they're consigned to, something they can't easily get out of.

Since that fateful evening in Washington, D.C., I've been thinking about commitment. Recently, Nichole said that she wants to explore having a fully committed relationship with me. Things have been so smooth and fun with her that my heart is filling with emotion and I feel like I want that as well. But there is that fear voice inside that stops me. That part of me has me convinced that I am not sure I am ready to move to full-on monogamy with her. So I told her, "For right now, let's just keep 'dating' and getting to know each other better." I knew I was saying the right words, but I also knew that I wasn't being honest about my own fears. It made me wonder why for some men and women, the very thought of commitment makes them feel like they're suffocating.

I once felt the pressure of a woman trying to conquer me. She was not trying to befriend me, and she was not necessarily trying to love me, but I knew that she was trying to conquer me. It was almost as if I was some strange, mysterious country, some sort of challenge. I have to say, the feeling that a partner is trying to possess or conquer you is pretty disturbing. It's almost guaranteed to make a man flee—or shut down.

A number of my female friends value "commitment," but what many of them mean when they say "commitment" is "fidelity." For me, commitment means so much more than simply not being with someone else. My friend Julia recently said to me, "I just want a man who won't cheat." And I thought, "Wow that's a low bar." I don't think that any of us should have to settle in choosing a partner. I think we have to be clear in identifying those things that we most want in a partner—is it just fidelity or is it fully formed commitment? If commitment is what we want, are we ready to "commit" to being joyous, full of life, engaging, positive, and fun? It seems that many men fear commitment because they don't want to end up with someone who thinks that they are fulfilling their commitment by simply not sleeping with someone else. All of us should want and bring so much more.

The other day, I was doing a little online reading, and I came across a really interesting article. It was reprinted from *Cosmopolitan* and titled "Why Guys Marry Some Girls (But Not Others)" by Beth Whiffen. The answers that were given were definitely not PC, but the validity of them would probably surprise a lot of women. In a nutshell, it said that there are five crucial traits that separate the women men date from the ones they eventually choose to marry.

Here's a quick breakdown of the traits (again, don't shoot the messenger):

⚘

Tie-the-Knot-Trait 1:
She's Exciting and Always Evolving

Tie-the-Knot-Trait 2:
She Really, Really Loves Sex

Tie-the-Knot-Trait 3:
She Makes It Clear He's Not Her Entire Life

Tie-the-Knot-Trait 4:
. . . Yet She Still Conveys How Very Important He Is to Her

Tie-the-Knot-Trait 5:

She Wants Him to Be the Best Man He Can Be

I brought up the idea of commitment and the traits listed in the article with my outspoken male friends to get their thoughts. We ended up discussing everything from commitment, to things women do that get on their nerves, to what makes them run for the hills.

The bottom line seems to be that each man varies in his desire or ability to happily commit. So do many women, though they tend not to admit it (at least, not to me—lol). It seems pretty clear that all of us should focus on being the best versions of ourselves. There is nothing that a woman *has* to do to get a man to commit. The man who sees that special spark in her, that only she possesses, will not expect her to be anything other than who she is. And he will value, appreciate, and love her for it.

BLACK MEN SPEAK II

Hill: Fellas, what do you think makes a man commit to one woman but not another?

Brad: This is a very complex question because every man has different reasons for committing. It just depends on what's going on in his life at that given time. Ultimately, I think the reasons a man will settle down are: (a) timing; (b) the woman befriended him; (c) the woman caters to his male ego; (d) the woman keeps him stimulated. Men are simple creatures. If she taps into her man, *a* through *d*, then she's got him.

Justin: It's easy. The chick he left he wasn't into . . . the next one he was; simple and done.

Jared: There is no rule to this. Men cannot control who they fall in love with. A man can be with the perfect woman who would kiss the ground he walks on but will not be able to commit to her if he isn't in love with her. I think that many times we have a *very* hard time breaking up with women that we have a lot of love for but are not in love with. We love them enough to not want to hurt them by breaking up with them but not enough to devote all of our attention to them. I guess what I'm saying is that it's *very* hard to break up with a woman that you don't hate!

Zee: In the words of Katt Williams, "You need to figure out what about your pussy keeps attracting ain't shit Brothas." It's really not deep. 'Cause basically, if a man didn't want you, then the exact reason why doesn't even matter. I think women need to quit crying and stop trying to figure old stuff out. Take a cue from the man who left you and *move the fuck on*.

David: Some women really need to learn and accept that you can't force a person to be in love with you or to marry you, no matter how long you stick around, if that person doesn't feel "it." And it also does not mean there is something wrong with you if your ex happens to find "it" with the next lady he has a relationship with. One has nothing to do with the other outcome.

Kyle: I tell any young dude willing to listen that you really should live with a woman for at least a year and get to know the real her before you commit to spending the rest of your life with her. Instead, we tend to commit for all the wrong reasons, and end up in relationships that fail as a result.

Eric: Folks make it sound like the human mind and its intent is some complicated stuff that needs to be debated ad nauseam. . . . No. . . . He left one woman because it just did not work out. Then he met someone else, liked her, and married her. Sorry, I think that is all there is to it.

Hill: What do you think we look for in deciding whether to commit or not?

Calvin: Experience is the best teacher. Even for men who use the "I don't see myself ever getting married" bomb, I have seen that a real good woman will change your mind in most cases. They will help you be a better person, but the whole concept of relationships is so mythological that we fall in love with the concept of love, not knowing what we really need in a partner. In my opinion, this is the main reason for so many failed marriages and way more failed relationships.

Greg: At the top of my list would be: How is she with kids? Is she humble enough to be in a long-term relationship? Because in my opinion, ego has killed ninety-five percent of relationships. Do we share the same values in life? The list goes on and on. But see, that is just my list. Men are more diverse than most people think. For example, I know some guys who like submissive women; some like a gangsta bitch; some need a pushy woman to lead them around because they have no backbone; some need a doormat to make them feel superior; and how about the guy who wants a White girl to show he has arrived (or that he will fake it till he make it); or the guy who is superreserved so he may want someone like himself; some men married their mama; others like Suzy homemaker; some can see a reflection of themselves in their significant others, which can be good or bad. The bottom line is that no one can predetermine what a man wants in a woman, even generally speaking, because I don't think most Black males really know what they want in a long-term relationship until they experience it firsthand. That is when they might say, this right here . . . is "the one." So, I hate to say it, but if he let you go without at least even attempting to lock it down, then you were not the one he is looking for.

Warren: This may sound corny, but it is true because I speak from my current experience. Everyone has someone out there for them; they just gotta find their match, and all the bullshit goes out the window. When that happens, the person you are with will love everything about you.

Hill: What are some things that get on your last nerves when you are dating or in a serious relationship with a woman?

Jared: I hate when a woman allows family and friends to get all in our business. I wish she would realize that there are many aspects of our lives that need to be just that—*ours*! It should be about us trying to work through our bad and enjoy our good. It should not be about them and what they continually think about us. Because if that's how you want it, okay, here, go have the relationship with them, because I'm out.

Brad: I have a lot of pet peeves. First and foremost, I am a neat freak. I cannot stand for anything to be out of place . . . clothes on the floor, dishes in the sink, dirty counters or tables, unmade beds, and most important, water all over the sink. I hate cat hair. . . . I'm allergic. I can't stand when a woman repeats herself over and over. I have a memory like an elephant. You don't have to tell me anything more than once. I don't like hypocrisy. . . . In other words, treat others like you want to be treated. If you ever do or say something to me that you have complained about being said or done to you, we have a problem. I don't like vicious mood swings either. It's one thing to be moody; it's another ball game when you get in your "funks" and you take it out on all the people who had nothing to do with pissing you off. Lastly (this is the one that gets me in trouble), please think about what you're going to say before you say it. Statements that come out as pure emotion, illogical and lacking rationality, really upset me. Once you say words to people, you cannot take back those words. Even with an apology, the words have forever entered the universe. Plus, I don't forget anything, so if she is talking irrationally . . . nine times out of ten, she will contradict herself. This is *the* biggest turnoff to me.

Chris: Honestly, I am beyond letting something get on my last nerves, but when I was younger I would say not being truthful. I guess I used to believe, "Tell it like it is, good, bad, and ugly." But again, I have learned there is a reason for everything, and when you have been married for a while you are attached to that person. So it's a matter of talking it out, being honest about how you feel, and not letting emotions drive your initial response, as it most times is not going to give you the desired outcome.

11.

Eros vs. Sex / Lust vs. Love

Love seeks to satisfy others at the expense of self. Lust seeks to satisfy self at the expense of others.

—Pastor A. R. Bernard,
married to Karen Bernard since 1978

In ancient Greece they had five different words for our one word *love*. They distinguished different senses or meanings: *agape*—pure or ideal love; *philia*—honorable love of community and friends; *storge*—love of a parent for a child; *xenia*—love expressed through hospitality to others; and finally *eros*—passionate, erotic, sexual love.

It's almost impossible to turn on a television or look at a magazine today without seeing something to do with eros. In fact, if I judged my sex life from what I see in music videos, I would think that I didn't have a very good one. If you listen to the song lyrics or watch the videos, you would think that Black folks are having good ol'-fashioned sex as much as, if not more than, any other group of people out there. But are we really? I'm not so sure about that.

I'm of the opinion that in our community, we are having more "sex" than *eros* ("good sex"). And now I have to define good sex. Good sex is (for me) empowered sex between partners who are where they want to be, doing what they want to do, on purpose and with a clear heart and a clear mind. It's uplifting, loving, and positive and in no way damaging, hurtful, or unhealthy.

I think open and honest communication about sex is critical, for both our happiness and our health. As a group, our inability to communicate about sex and sexuality has led to the highest rates of teen pregnancy and the greatest number of children born out of wedlock in the nation, as well as the fastest-growing rates of HIV/AIDS infection of any distinct group.

A study from the University of Texas at Austin reports that when two thousand people were interviewed about their sex lives, they gave 237 reasons for having sex, ranging from the very funny to the deeply serious. The reasons included: "I wanted a job"; "I wanted to change the topic of conversation"; "I was afraid my partner would have an affair if I didn't"; and "I wanted to feel loved." There is so much politics surrounding sex and sexuality that it is difficult for sex to be a place of empowerment and honesty.

I think this is particularly true in the Black community. The dominant culture has projected assumptions of promiscuity upon Black women, and in response many Black women have chosen to stay in a locked-down mode. Within the Black community, some men say that Black women are frigid because they are so uncomfortable in their bodies. Which is true? Are Black women promiscuous or frigid? The answer of course is both and neither.

The bigger issue is that these labels prevent women from defining their sexuality for themselves. Black men have been called (and we even call ourselves) "pimps" and "playas," and not so long ago we were treated like studs (in the farm-animal sense, not in the "he's so hot, he's so sexy" sense). Some men feel ego empowerment by big displays of their sexuality, bragging about how many kids they have and how much sex they are getting. But some Black men who are not sexually aggressive have told me that they have been accused of being on the "down low." There is not a lot of clarity for us around sex. The biggest problem is that we are not defining our sexuality for ourselves and instead are projecting on each other what the dominant culture projects on us. No matter the context, if we fail to define ourselves, we will live by other people's definitions of us.

What would empowerment look like? There are so many women who, instead of loving their beautiful bodies, seem to be in love with the idea of what their bodies can get them. Men complain about the way women use sex as a bargaining tool and the way women deny men sex when they want to punish them. But all of these statements assume that women do not enjoy sex. This is the opposite of sexual empowerment.

For the rest of this chapter, I am going to lay a bunch of ideas and issues on the table. I've always been interested in what I see around me, so I've got a lot of questions, and I hope a few answers.

It seems to me that the basic things we want are pretty clear. A man wants to find a woman who wants to be with him. A woman wants to find a man who wants to be with her. They each want to find someone they like. They want to come together in a good spirit, and they want to enjoy talking and spending time with each other. And it seems safe to say that they both want to enjoy each other's bodies and be enjoyed by the other in the act of sex. So far, so good—it all sounds pretty simple. So why does it break down? *Where* does it break down?

We can start trying to answer those questions by looking to our bodies, the very tools that we use in the act of sex, to give us some clues. Did you know that there is a hormone called oxytocin that is released by both men and women during sex? Oxytocin is called the "bonding hormone" because it is secreted into women's bloodstreams during breast-feeding to bond mother to baby. Oxytocin is responsible for the feel-good feeling we all get when we cuddle or have an orgasm. But here is the trick: Women's bodies secrete oxytocin more often than men's bodies do, and women have more receptors in their bodies for the hormone. What does this mean? It means that every act of affection or sex is more biologically significant to a woman. Her biology has set her up to bond with every human who causes the release of this hormone. While the hormone may be active in a man's body for up to three hours after a physical encounter, the larger number of receptors in a woman's body can keep the hormone active in her system for as long as three days.

Guys, take note: When a woman is all dreamy and bright eyed after sex because (you think) you rocked her world, her body chemistry is telling her to bond with you. Her mind, however, may be trying to figure out whether or not she even likes you enough to do it again. For women, that sensation of intimacy and vulnerability remains for days. That's how strong oxytocin is. It's important for men to be aware of this effect and to take responsibility for it. A woman is not stalking you simply because she expects you to call the next day. She wants to know that you respect the intimacy that the two of you shared, not to mention the fact that when a man and a woman have intercourse it is the woman that is bringing the man into her. A man's body is not entered by the woman. That difference alone creates a different level of intimate interaction. Some male friends have told me that sometimes sex for them is no more intimate than masturbation.

What sex is to men is often very different from what it is to women. The evidence is everywhere, from the differences in our biology to the different ways we use language. Studies show that women often suggest sex as a shorthand for closeness. A woman might suggest to a man that they get together, and he might assume that this means he will get some sex. She, however, might want romantic time with him (no sex implied); she might want to cuddle with him (sex is possible but not her goal); perhaps she wants more intimacy in the sex they will be having (a shift from just "doing it" to making love); or maybe she just wants sex. For a man, often sex means sex. If he signs on for sex and gets rocked by the bonding hormone, it's gravy.

When a man initiates sex, it is not necessarily to feel closer to his partner. For him, the sexual experience might be a way to experience the feeling he gets from going for a run, or driving a fast car, or seeing a movie, or doing any other activity that offers pleasurable sensations. In short, a man may initiate sex for no other reason than the enjoyment of the physical experience that sex is, and this can come into conflict with the emotions the woman may bring to the experience. He might enjoy the pleasure of her company, but what she hears may not be what he is saying. For a good number of men, sex is pure carnal pleasure. It releases stress and allows them to feel good. I had one friend tell me, "I like to have sex when I go to bed because it helps me fall asleep easier."

When women expect sex to be the doorway into a relationship, it leaves them at cross-purposes with men and can contribute to the communication breakdown. Neither is saying what he or she means—not on purpose, but because it hasn't occurred to the person that his or her partner means something else when he or she uses the same words. How can we expect things to get better if we are not willing to make our truth known to the person we are having sexual relations with?

Let's talk about hidden agendas. Men are confused by women saying one thing while meaning another. Some women think men should read their minds and decipher what they really mean. Alternatively, they give the answer society or their mother told them was the proper answer, though it may not be their truth at all. For instance, a number of my female friends truly love and enjoy great, passionate, and adventurous sex, but for some reason, when they're with the men they date, they don't express to them any of their own passion. They think "good girls" don't do that and that the man should always initiate anything new or "adventurous."

I do realize that there are a number of women who don't necessarily know what they want or how to ask for it. I am not trying to say that women are deliberately obtuse, but men are simple creatures and they do want women to be pleased (for their egos, if nothing else), so if a woman has the courage to be an enthusiastic, positive trainer, a man who is worth her time will do everything and anything she wants him to. And the big bonus is: He will like her more because he will sense that she enjoys sex (with him). Everybody wins! What's most important to me is that all of us, men and women, have the courage to be completely ourselves, even in the most intimate contexts.

Part of the problem is that women are sent so many different messages—by their upbringing, by men, by the media and pop culture, as well as by professional environments—that it's hard to figure out who to be and what to pay attention to. There is an old adage that says "a woman

> ❧
> **Be completely yourself.**
> ❧

should be a chef in the kitchen, a lady in public, and a whore in the bedroom," but if you were all those things, how would you represent yourself? This is a uniquely female problem. Look again at the statement. There is no male equivalent in which a man is required to be all things to the world, or even only to the woman in his life. We as men are the ones responsible for putting all of that on women, and we need to stop. For women, the issue of finding a healthy balance between all that is expected of her can be a tiring lifelong quest.

To make matters worse, consider the way some men view women. The Madonna/whore complex, in which women are seen as being either one or the other, is a pernicious trap. A man may feel that the woman who is most appropriate for him is a Madonna, but in this false construct, Madonnas cannot be sexually exciting, so the man seeks out other women for the purpose of expressing his sexuality while his wife waits at home having no fun and not getting good sex. Or if the Madonna he's dating wants to try something new in the bedroom, he suddenly decides she's a whore. It is this lack of clarity and these insecurities among both men and women around sex that keep us all living in our hall of mirrors. The man with the Madonna/whore complex needs to get over it and communicate more openly and honestly with the *one* he is with. In the same way, the woman who may not enjoy sex with the guy she's dating but pretends she does, while at the same time not wanting to seem too promiscuous, is on a slippery slope. We all need to get out of the hall of mirrors and have the courage to be ourselves—fully and authentically.

The reality for most women is that their love for or disinterest in sex is very specific to the guy involved. They can love sex with one guy and be bored or just not turned on by another. Sex is no doubt very complicated, which is all the more reason communication is critical. Take, for example, something my friend Gail said to me when we were hiking together in the Hollywood Hills. "Hill, he's just not a good lover . . . but I like him and I don't want to bruise his ego." There is no question that a lot of men haven't learned how to please a woman (just as there are many women who haven't learned how to please a man—just because a man had an orgasm doesn't necessarily mean the sex was great for him). In Gail's case, she was not enjoying the sex but liked her man and was afraid to hurt his feelings by telling him she wasn't getting turned on. A woman can really, really like a guy even though he leaves her cold in the bedroom; the reverse can also be true: An inappropriate "bad boy" may be so hot she can't get enough sex, even though she knows he's not right for her.

Yes, it's complicated, and things can get very conflicted. Many women say they want a sensitive and loving man, but studies on body language have shown that women are more attracted to alpha males. So the brotha who has perfected his swagger and knows how to take control has a better chance of getting laid.

Can you see what a mess this is?

This is what I think: At its best, sex has the power to show a completely different side of who we are to our partners. When we are speaking face-to-face in a conversation, there are real limits to what we can convey, even if we talk all day, scream at the top of our lungs, and laugh with each other as we share our ideas and experiences.

> ❧
> **Be friends first.**
> ❧

All that is great, but it is only during sex that we really get to *feel* each other—and that is exciting and beautiful. I would hope for everyone to be wide open to the possibility of sex as a powerful and expressive part of their relationship. In order for that to happen, though, there has to be trust, fun, and ease—in other words, friendship. The only way to arrive at these vital preconditions is through communication. Expanding boundaries and opening up the definition of what sex can be should be the goal between two consenting adults—to put all that feeling, desire, lust, and emotion out there into the sex they are having. That to me is good sex. That to me is *eros*.

But wait! The conversation about sex is not over just yet. There are practical and detailed aspects of having sex that have to be discussed out in the open—before the act—in order to make sure you're on the same page as your partner and to move your relationship forward in a healthy way.

> ❧
> **Make sure you're on the same page as your partner.**
> ❧

PREMARITAL SEX

Many people assume they will eventually engage in sexual activity with their partner when they've reached a certain comfort level in their relationship. There are some people, though, who believe that no matter what level of comfort they feel in a relationship, the appropriate time to have sex is after marriage. Whether it's for religious reasons or their own personal convictions, premarital sex is simply not an option for these people.

The time to express these beliefs is not when you're in bed together making out and touching, with your partner thinking that intercourse will follow. This discussion deserves to be had without the distraction of sexual desire looming overhead. It might end up being a deal breaker in a relationship—if one person feels that it places too much pressure on him or her to commit to marriage—or it might end up being a plus, offering both of you a new way to explore and get to know each other in an intimate yet nonsexual way. Whatever the result, you owe it to yourself, your partner, and your relationship to have the conversation in a serious way.

CONTRACEPTION

It never ceases to amaze me how many times I've heard people say that they thought the other person would be responsible for protection. Some men feel that if a woman doesn't say anything about contraception or ask him to wear a condom, she has it all under control. They assume she's on the pill, and then they get the shock of their lives when they discover weeks later that the woman is pregnant. Then they claim that they were being tricked, that the woman was trying to get pregnant all along.

I've also heard men tell me that if they meet a woman who carries her own condoms, then that means she's promiscuous— and we are right back in the hall of mirrors again. I would view a woman who carried condoms as someone who is intelligent and cared about her own health and safety as well as the health and safety of her partner—a plus, not a minus. Men need to re-member that since women take us in, they are more susceptible to all of the negative effects that can come from unprotected sex, whether it's pregnancy or STDs. When we look at it that way, it's almost odd that we live in a society in which the purchase and marketing of condoms is focused on men. Not surprisingly, it is men who control the advertising companies and men who are sometimes intimidated by a woman's sexual empowerment.

We've been so conditioned by television and movies to think of sex as something romantic that just happens, a feeling that sweeps us up and guides our actions, that we forget things don't always happen that way in real life. Sure, we can get swept up in the moment, but we still have to deal with real-world feet-on-the-ground issues like protection. When facing an unplanned pregnancy, you've got to consider, would it have killed the mood *that much* to ask whether you should put on a condom?

The thing we have to remember about being swept up in the moment is that it's only a moment. We have to think about the rest of our lives. According to the Centers for Disease Control and Prevention, the highest rates of STDs in the United States are found in the Black community. In 2005, we were eighteen times as likely as Whites to have gonorrhea and about five times as likely to have syphilis. It's also estimated that as many as one in four Blacks have genital herpes, which is a lifelong viral infection, yet up to 90 percent of those with herpes are unaware that they have it. Those are just the diseases that are not life threatening if treated.

More disturbingly, HIV/AIDS has reached epidemic propor-tions in the Black community. Black women are being infected with HIV/AIDS more rapidly than any other demographic group in the country. It is now the number one killer of Black women between the ages of twenty and twenty-five. For these women—

our lovers, sisters, best friends, mothers, and even daughters—the primary means of infection is through high-risk heterosexual contact. If you are a Black woman reading this who engages in any kind of heterosexual activity, this statistic represents you. Safety and protection when having sex are more than important. They are a matter of life and death. That's why, if you choose to be sexually active, gender-based notions of who should or should not be buying or carrying condoms are ridiculous.

When the time is right, we should try to incorporate the discussion of sex into our conversations with potential partners. Notice, I said *conversations*, plural. I don't believe that sex should be this mysterious activity that we just do and don't ever talk about. By talking about it, I don't mean having phone sex; I mean talking about it in the same way that we talk about anything else that's important to our future.

In addition to finding out what my partner's general views are on sex, I want to know what type of contraception she prefers and whether she has any health concerns I should know about. For example, many people with the herpes virus are able to have a relatively normal, healthy sex life, but it's important for their partners to know this about them and for them to take steps together to ensure that their partners do not become infected as well. It's up to both parties to create a safe space for honest communication.

I get tested for HIV/AIDS regularly and require that my partner also get tested. If you choose to be sexually active, it is an essential habit to have. Once, my girlfriend and I decided to get tested together. Even though she had been tested just six months earlier, and I had been tested only a couple of months before, we went to the clinic together and got tested again. While we were waiting for our test results, a counselor talked to us in a private office about risk factors and safe-sex practices. The whole process was a shared experience that brought us closer together.

> ❧
> Honest communication is a matter of life or death.
> ❧

SEXUAL EXPERIMENTATION AND COMPATIBILITY

We all have some idea of what we are and are not open to when it comes to sex, and it's good to communicate that with your partner. Over the years, several of my female friends have told me stories about dating men who wanted and accepted fellatio but refused to perform cunnilingus. For some, that was a deal breaker. They just couldn't imagine spending another ten minutes in bed, let alone a whole lifetime, with someone who would not go down on them. I've had male friends who've expressed the same frustration with girlfriends who would not "return the favor."

Some forms of compatibility will be revealed only during sex. More than a few of my friends have said, "Our bodies just fit well together," when I've asked them what it is about their sexual life with their partner that makes it so fulfilling. But some things can be discussed beforehand.

The point is not to make a partner feel bad for what he or she wants or does, but to make sure that you both want and are willing to do the same things. Good sex is a healthy part of a good relationship. It's understandable that a lot of people feel uncomfortable about their sexuality, because it's not something that we're taught how to speak about openly, directly, and in detail. In fact, it's something that we spend a good part of our upbringing being taught not to talk about. But couples who treat sex as an important part of their relationship and strive to achieve the best sex life they possibly can are well on their way to a long-lasting relationship.

PORN

A few years ago I starred in a romantic comedy called *Love, Sex and Eating the Bones*. In the film, my character, who is addicted to porn, falls for a professional sister who is celibate. In doing research for the role (yes, I did research; don't laugh) I found many people who enjoyed "sex DVDs" but hated to use the word *porn*. They said it just sounded "dirty."

If you discover that your man is into Internet porn or DVDs, here is what it does *not* mean:

1. It does not mean that he is not into you.
2. It does not mean that he needs help (unless what he is viewing is criminal).
3. It does not mean that he is not in love with you.
4. It does not mean that he is unfaithful.
5. It does not mean that he has a problem (unless, like my character in the movie, it's almost all he does).

Sex DVDs, or porn, are simply a tool for sexual arousal and enjoyment. They are similar to sex toys or vibrators or "motion lotions," or role playing, or any number of options available to *encourage* pleasure, alone or with a partner. There is nothing wrong with two consenting adults enjoying a walk on the wild side. There are now millions of women who watch porn with their mates. I know couples who go to "sex stores" together, and they have healthy, monogamous sexual relationships. Today, there is even porn geared specifically toward women that includes a storyline and interesting characters. Most men want a woman to have an open mind about their sexual interests. And it's equally important for a woman to share her interests and desires as well. As I said earlier, I have some friends who explore and discover porn together, but I also have friends who feel they have to keep their interests a secret from their mate. That can't be good for their relationships. Our sexual fantasies don't need to be another way that we are not communicating. They shouldn't turn into secrets, which in turn can start to feel like lies, and add a level of estrangement to our relationship. Imagine this conversation:

Woman: Honey, I want to know what you like. I'm your wife.

Many men would respond, "You are exactly what I like," when the completely true response might be:

Man: Well, recently I've kinda been looking at some sex DVDs and I was hoping maybe you'd watch some with me?

He'd like to hear her respond with something like:

Woman: Porn? I don't know . . . but I'm willing to give it a try.

But maybe he's afraid of hearing something like this:

Woman: Porn? That is disgusting. I'm not watching a bunch of skinny White women get some brother off.

Man: No, it's not like that anymore. The people look like us. Come on, give it a try? It might turn you on.

(Woman gives him a glare.)

Woman: I am not watching porn. You need to get to church and get right with God.

Man: Baby, you asked me, and I was just tryin' to tell you.

Woman: I didn't know it was going to be something as nasty as porn.

(He tries to soothe her.)

Woman: Get your nasty hands off of me.

(She leaves. He goes into his study, locks the door, and starts browsing the Internet for porn.)

This example may seem a little extreme; however, it is a real conversation described to me by one of the married men I interviewed for this book. I recognize that the above exchange is from the man's point of view, and certainly there are plenty of women who enjoy porn and enjoy it with their husbands and boyfriends. Maybe his wife had never been exposed to porn; all she knew was that she had been told it was bad. But how is this couple ever going to be able to talk openly about sex again? Their conversation has been killed before it even got started.

I think both men and women could work harder to create a safe space for communication, and I believe that this is even more critical for Black couples because of the historical stigmas and stereotypes surrounding Black male and female sexuality that serve to hinder our communication that much more.

My point here is less about porn and more about the problems we're having with the conversation. I'm not advocating porn. I am simply keeping it real and using porn as an example, because there are a number of men who enjoy watching sex films. We have to be able to talk about all kinds of things, without fear of attack or judgment. That's the only way the conversation is going to work.

12.

Cheating: *Reindeer Games*

———— ❧ ————

I never worry about things I can't affect and with fidelity . . .
that is between Barack and me, and if somebody can come between us,
we didn't have much to begin with.

—First Lady Michelle Obama,
married to President Barack Obama since 1992

I bet the instant you read the title of this chapter, a whole lot of you immediately assumed that this part of the conversation would be about men. I can't say I blame you; you're not alone. When you're talking about a relationship and you say "cheater," most people automatically assume the cheater is the man. For whatever reason, people are more inclined to believe that men are not genetically programmed toward monogamy and that it is in their nature to cheat. Probably because of that, there is a much greater stigma attached to women who commit adultery than there is to men. Women who cheat are considered wanton and unladylike. Men are "just being men." But if we're going to have a real conversation here, we've got to get past stereotypes and recognize that men and women are both capable of being unfaithful.

Now that we've got that out of the way, let me ask a question: Is flirting the same thing as cheating? Before you answer, let me tell you a couple of quick stories. The first one, I'm not proud to say, is about me. And yes, it involves Nichole. I messed up bad.

Just Couldn't Help Myself

A few weeks ago, Nichole came to L.A. for a few days to visit me and do a teacher's seminar. One night I took her to a sexy lounge called Hyde, where a number of models and actors go out for drinks. As I was walking to the bar to get Nichole a glass of wine, I looked across the room and a beautiful sistah was staring right at me. Every relationship has markers that can change its course, and this could have been one, because in a moment of stupidity, I politely nodded to her as I headed to the bar. Right after I arrived she was standing right next to me. In her defense, she did not see me sitting with Nichole; as far as she knew, I wasn't with anyone. And I have to admit, I was attracted to her, but in my mind I was thinking, *How can I be attracted to another woman when Nichole is sitting right over there?*

I am the first to admit that I am not a perfect man, and as we spoke, as I waited for the wine, I had convinced myself that it was fine to speak to her because I was making a new "friend." Yeah, right. Just as I was paying I made another incredibly stupid decision. I said, "You should give me your number; we'll stay in touch." Just as we were exchanging numbers, Nichole walked up. *Damn*, I thought, *why couldn't I avoid just one woman for one night for the sake of my current blissful developing relationship?* But, hey, officially I was still single, or maybe I was just self-sabotaging again. Anyway, the look on Nichole's face made me feel horrible. I had hurt someone I cared about, and I knew I had to make more changes and difficult choices.

Just a "Friend"

Trina is a friend of a friend. Trina and her husband, Anthony, had been married for about three years, and they had a two-year-old daughter. Neither Trina nor Anthony would've said that there was anything really wrong with their marriage. Anthony thought it was perfect, holding steady. Trina thought it was pleasant enough but also a bit boring and predictable.

She had married Anthony because she loved him. He was dependable, gentle, and considerate, and he was a good provider. But he wasn't the most exciting man Trina had ever gone out with, not that she'd mention that to Anthony. After all, she loved him. One evening while Trina and Anthony were at a party at a friend's house, Trina struck up a conversation with one of the other guests, a married man named Jeff. They realized they lived not far from each other, and so they exchanged numbers. Trina promised to have him and his wife over to visit her and Anthony.

On the way home from the party, Trina told Anthony all about Jeff and the conversation they'd had. She left out the part about flirting with him and how alive that had made her feel. That evening, Trina and Anthony made love for the first time in a long while.

The following day, Jeff texted Trina. The two of them started e-mailing and texting back and forth. They became Facebook friends and within three weeks started speaking on the phone regularly. Their conversations, texts, and e-mails became more and more frequent. After a while, they started getting together fairly often. He'd meet her in the park for a walk, sometimes pushing the baby stroller for her when she got tired. They'd meet for lunch and sit at the restaurant for hours. They talked about everything, from their problems to their goals, and sometimes their conversations and texts were teasing and flirtatious. Even though it was all "innocent," Trina never mentioned any of this to Anthony.

One afternoon, when Trina had just come back from a walk with Jeff, our mutual friend Mary stopped by. Trina told Mary about her new friendship with Jeff.

"Friendship?" Mary said. "That's not a friendship. You're having an affair." Of course Trina adamantly denied it. How could she be having an affair when she'd never even kissed the man? "This isn't about sex," Mary replied, and continued, "How do you think Anthony would feel if you told him that while he was at work, you were spending your afternoons with another man, telling him your deepest secrets?"

Just No Secrets

Then there's my old friend Don, who loves to flirt and, as if to justify it, always follows it up with a statement I've heard men say my whole life: "I'm married, not dead."

When Don sees a woman he thinks is beautiful, he will not hesitate to let her know it. He'll walk up to her and strike up a conversation, making sure to compliment her on her hair, her smile, her clothing. If one of his buddies is with him, he'll introduce him to the woman and then start trying to play matchmaker. If it's just him, he'll generally ask her where she got her dress or her shoes or whatever other article of clothing or piece of jewelry he's complimented her on.

"I'd love to get that for my wife," he'll say to her, and then somehow, he'll manage to turn the conversation to Robin. If Don and the woman end up talking for a long time, by the end of it all, he will have told her how he and Robin met, what she does, what her interests are. And he will have exchanged numbers with the woman, with the promise of inviting her over for dinner.

One time, I asked Robin if she minded Don's flirting.

"Are you kidding?" She laughed. "I love it. He's got the best taste in women. He ends up meeting all these fly sistahs and he finds out where they get their shoes and purses and whatnot. That's how I got half my wardrobe—and half of my best girl-friends."

It's not the flirting that's the problem; it's the secrets. The problem with what Trina was doing was that she was talking only to Jeff about her problems, not Anthony. What makes Don's flirtations nonthreatening to his relationship is that he and Robin communicate openly about the people they meet when they are apart. They then introduce each other to the people they've become friends with.

Would Robin be hurt if she found out that Don had been getting together—even just platonically—with a woman regularly without letting her know? Yes.

Sharing that type of emotional intimacy with a person other than your spouse will eventually undermine a relationship. By the time Anthony got home from work, Trina had nothing to offer him by way of conversation. She had shared everything with Jeff. As time wore on, this drove a wedge between Trina and Anthony. He was no longer her primary relationship, and as a result, she didn't even feel comfortable being with him sexually. Their marriage slowly turned into a business relationship, and eventually they separated. It all started with what I like to call the "sexless affair."

But that's not what most folks think of when they hear the word *affair*. They think of one that involves the "other woman," or "other man." They think of clandestine meetings in seedy motels, lies about staying late at the office or traveling for business, unexplained charges to the credit card.

Those types of affairs generally fall into two categories. There are the one-time affairs. They are explained as a moment of weakness, something that began and ended with that single act, a lapse in judgment that will not be repeated. Then there are the long, drawn-out affairs, the ones that take place over a period of weeks, months, or even years. These are full-on relationships. Sometimes these relationships are even "open secrets," meaning that everyone knows about them but turns a blind eye to them and keeps their mouths shut. Everyone, that is, except the spouse.

I have had friends who've been shocked to discover that their spouses were cheating on them. My friend Boswell had no idea whatsoever that Lacy, his wife, and Chuck, one of his best friends, had been having an affair for nearly two years right under his nose. Boswell knew that whenever he'd travel, Chuck would check in on Lacy. He figured that the two of them were probably hanging out, drinking some wine, and watching TV or talking. He never for a second suspected that they were sleeping together, in his bed, in his home.

Boswell might not have known, but the rest of us had pretty much figured it out. Chuck and Lacy were not especially discreet. They had been seen at restaurants, at the movies, and out at the mall. People started talking, but no one said a word to

Boswell. Who would want that job? He ended up hearing about it from Lacy and Chuck, though they didn't plan for it to happen that way. Lacy knocked over her purse while she was with Chuck. Something in her purse must have knocked up against the talk button on her cell phone and made it redial Boswell, the last person she'd spoken to. When Boswell answered the call, he was able to hear them together in what was clearly a compromising situation.

A lot of my female friends have also told me about meeting and dating men who are on the down low—that is, men who front as heterosexuals but are actually gay and actively involved with other men. They are unwilling to give up the trappings of heterosexual privilege, and so they create artificial lives to mask who they really are.

The thing about these artificial lives is that the women they date or marry believe these lives to be quite real, and they invest in them accordingly. They put everything into their relationships, believing that they have found a man who will be with them for the long haul, a man who will love them and stay with them forever. Unbeknownst to them, the men are leading secret lives—with men, their *real* significant others.

Nothing a cheater will say can lessen the blow of knowing your trust has been betrayed. Honesty, trust, and friendship in a relationship are crucial, and no relationship can survive without them. Once they have been broken, you must ask the question of whether you will ever be able to trust that person again.

The question of whether a relationship can be rebuilt or whether it should be ended after an affair is an individual one. After a year of couples counseling and meetings with their pastor, Anthony was able to forgive Trina for her "sexless affair."

Boswell was not able to forgive Lacy or Chuck. He cut both of them out of his life completely.

> ⚜
> The roles that honesty and trust play in a relationship are crucial.
> ⚜

A recent study by relationship expert Gary Neuman showed that one in three men cheat during their marriage—and most of their wives don't know about it. In the study, 92 percent of men said the reason they cheated wasn't primarily about sex. "The majority said it was an emotional disconnection, specifically a sense of feeling underappreciated. A lack of thoughtful gestures," Neuman says. "Men are very emotional beings. They just don't look like that. Or they don't seem like that. Or they don't tell you that."

I do not want to condone cheating. I dated someone who cheated on me, and it was one of the worst pains I have experienced. It felt like my heart, my whole understanding of reality, and sometimes my very mind, was literally shattered into thousands of pieces.

There are many men (two out of three married men, according to Neuman's study) who experience the pride, joy, and excitement of flying high with one partner. However, the sad fact is that a lot of men do not have the willpower or even the desire to fight off temptation. There are many men who feel just as Chris Rock joked: "A man is only as faithful as his options."

In my business I am presented with many "options," and I can say that in some cases I have been completely faithful and in other cases . . . not as much. What was the difference? The multiple options were the same, but I learned in cases where I didn't stray that it wasn't as much about the woman I was with as about not putting myself in situations where I was vulnerable to temptation. My grandfather used to tell me, "If you don't want to get shot, don't go where the bullets are." I believe that's a good lesson for fidelity. And we all have to learn exactly what our own individual bullets are.

My bullets have much more to do with privacy than anything else. Up until the incident with Nichole, I felt that I could be around many incredibly beautiful single women in public and never do or say anything inappropriate, or get into an inappropriate situation. However, if I invite one to my hotel room, even if I think we are just going to "watch a movie and eat," then I'm in my bullet territory. You may say, "Yeah, that's obvious," but that's not true. The "bullet" moment for some men may be the second they are at dinner or the bar with an attractive female; for others, they may not be in bullet territory in private watching a movie or having a drink with someone. Women have their bullet thresholds as well. Being faithful takes some discipline and thought about one's future. In many ways, I guess it's a lot like saving and investing money—you may want to spend it now, but if you save and invest, it will exponentially grow, and the happiness you will have in the future will be compounded with interest. I think it's worth it!

For a long time I used to view "cheating" more from the standpoint of whether I broke a covenant with the person I was in a relationship with. I would always run to justifications like "Technically we were able to date other people" or, like Trina, "We never even

> Cheating is about how it makes your partner feel.

kissed; just some innocent flirtation." But cheating isn't just about the covenant broken or upheld; it's about how our actions make another person feel. And that's why I hope Nichole will forgive me for what happened at the bar. I was wrong and I knew better. I offered her a truly heartfelt apology. But I still wasn't sure whether it meant that she had lost trust that I could be monogamous. I hope not. I hope we will be able to get back on track, building the friendship that we started at the Blakes'.

I asked some of my guy friends to share their stories and advice on cheating—and find out some possible reasons why men (and women) cheat. I also wanted to know whether cheating has ever affected their relationships.

BLACK MEN SPEAK III

Hill: All right, let's get right to it, brothas. Why do some men cheat?

Eric: Most of the time it's because the other woman is offering something that his woman can't or won't. Think the eighty-twenty rule. It's true. And many times men choose to explore the twenty even when they got the eighty at home. It's not smart. It's selfish. The end.

Brad: Men cheat if they are not getting the same elements that ultimately make a man decide to commit and settle down with one woman. These elements are: timing; the woman befriended him; the woman caters to his male ego; or the woman keeps him stimulated. Ironic, isn't it? What can I say? Again, we men are simple creatures.

Ty: Sometimes it is because the outside woman is actually fulfilling that brotha's fantasy and giving him all that he feels his nagging, whining girlfriend or wife at home isn't. It's a getaway . . . like a mini-vacation.

Chris: Because we think it is easy, and society makes it easy. Again, most images are on the man stepping out, and often it is accepted, as the woman "stands by her man." So it just seems the consequences for our actions are less than if a woman does it.

Khalil: Women are gonna hate this, but there is no reason; it just is. It doesn't matter what the other female looked like, had, has, is, or whatever. And it isn't always some ugly woman that is relegated to be the side chick either. Here's a novel thought: maybe some people just cheat. It's kind of like asking some explorers why they climbed Mount Everest. The bottom line is this: Men will cheat because of space and opportunity, and women will cheat because of feelings of insecurity.

Justin: Cheating is a simple thing. It really doesn't need any serious in-depth conversation or understanding. People cheat because of selfish reasons. Period. It ain't about if she ugly or cuter than you. Dude just said fuck it and did what he wanted to do. Period. Some men come into the relationship cheating and never stop. They sexing just to be sexin'. You just happen to catch the dude. But don't mean she's the only one. At the end of the day, this is a character question, nothing more or less. Either men will be faithful and keep it one hundred, or they just creep and lie until they get caught. Then they will usually make up some shit, cry a little bit, beg a little bit, most of the time the women they deal with will take them back, and then guess what? They go and do the same exact shit again. It's funny to me, 'cause in the end it is on the woman if you keep staying with that dude.

Jared: Men cheat because they are horny. Nothing more, nothing less!

Zee: Ah, man, do they really want to know? It's simple . . . ain't no pussy better than new pussy. And that's something only a man will ever be able to fully understand.

Hill: Given what you just said, do you guys think that people—men in particular—can really be faithful and monogamous?

Brad: Absolutely. People who are fulfilled have no reason to stray. Period.

Jared: Of course they can! I've been faithful in two of my relationships! If you decide to be faithful, you'll be faithful. Simple as that. It's just like quitting smoking.

Chris: I think so. If you are open and honest about your needs, wants, and desires, you can keep it fresh and new and ensure friendship. I always say we can keep good friends forever; why can't we do the same with our spouses? But that said, I do know that some men just can't do it, so it is what it is. But as a man, you have to know that about yourself and be honest with yourself as well as that woman. And women need to be careful about thinking they can change a man's behaviors and actions. Whether you are the man or the woman in the situation, just don't fool yourself, because we normally don't change who we really are.

Hill: Chris, you just reminded me of something Oprah said: "When people show you who they are, *believe them*."

13.

Complicating Matters

My toughest fight was with my first wife.

—Muhammad Ali,
married to his fourth wife, Yolanda Ali, since 1986

When my friends and I were in our twenties and dating pretty heavily, we made it a point to avoid getting involved with women who were divorced or had children. Even though we were considered adults by then, none of us felt that way. Few of us had our acts together. We were still trying to figure out how to translate those college degrees into real jobs, and still trying to find our place in the real world. There was something intimidating about meeting women with all that life experience. They made us feel like boys—people who weren't ready to handle the responsibility of being men.

I had a buddy, though, who ended up in a committed relationship with a woman who already had a child. While my

friends and I looked at the situation and saw complications, he saw all the right pieces to a perfect future.

By the time I hit my midthirties, it seemed as though every other woman I met had children or an ex-husband or both, and I started to realize that all of us come with complications, whether we are married or single, parents or childless. Some of us have demanding careers. Being on the road all the time or working an eighty-hour-a-week job doesn't leave much room for relaxation, let alone a relationship. Some of us come with a houseful of pets or strange, dysfunctional relatives. All of a sudden, kids didn't seem like such a big deal.

This isn't to say that dating someone who has an ex-husband, an ex-wife, or children doesn't bring on a new set of obstacles. These situations are nontraditional. We may meet a wonderful brotha or sistah who has experienced the death of his or her spouse; or lives across the country; or comes from a completely different ethnic background. Each of these scenarios requires extra care—whether it's a willingness to achieve a deeper understanding of the other person's experiences, making the time for cross-country iChats, or dealing with people who might not understand your decision to date outside your race. The bottom line is that we can't predict who is going to come along and knock us right off our feet. After all, you don't always choose love—sometimes love chooses you. When you meet the right person, your perspective shifts and judgments just disappear.

DATING A DIVORCÉ

Given the current statistics, chances are good that if you're of dating age, you'll meet someone who is divorced, a single parent, or both. According to recent data from the U.S. Census Bureau, 33.4 percent of first marriages end in divorce before their fifteenth anniversary. The data also indicate that well over 50 percent of Black children live in single-parent families headed by the mother.

People who have been divorced have already decided that they wanted to share the rest of their lives with someone. For whatever reason, the marriage did not work. You've probably heard the expression "once bitten, twice shy." Some divorced people are resistant to the idea of falling in love and getting married again. They don't think marriage works, or they don't want to risk getting hurt in the same way they have been.

A person's views on marriage after divorce will have a lot to do with the cause of his or her divorce. If it was infidelity, then he or she might have issues of trust. If it was because the two grew apart as a couple, then she or he might require closer communication in future relationships. Whatever the case may be, it's important to be sensitive and patient, to discuss his or her fears, and to be respectful of whatever additional time the person may need before taking the plunge, so to speak. I

> I like the idea of practicing patience with passion.

like the idea of practicing patience with passion.

Dealing with the former spouse can be trying at times. It can be hard to find that balance between being your partner's confidant and just staying the heck out of it. It's not always clear what your role is. It's important to remember not to rush it. Your role will reveal itself through time, not through your insistence.

DATING WITH KIDS

A few years ago, I dated an amazing woman with an incredible son. We became very serious. We were both actors, so our schedules were erratic and I was concerned about how her having the additional commitment of her son would affect our relationship. I was so surprised by what actually happened. I soon realized that her being a mom actually *helped* our relationship. Number one, it forced us both to make and keep plans with each other and not take each other for granted in any way. Since we didn't have a lot of casual time, we were living proof of the saying "You should never spend serious time with casual people." It also allowed our relationship to evolve at its own pace. Since she already had a child, her biological clock wasn't ticking. She didn't feel that we had to have the "Where is this going? . . . I can't afford to waste any time" conversation too early.

Dating a parent means that your relationship affects and is affected by the needs of individuals other than you and your partner. This might mean that your relationship will have certain limitations. For example, your partner may not be available on the weekends he or she has the children. Or your partner might be the primary caretaker and be available only on the weekends that the other parent has the children, which is something that we must remember and respect.

There are a lot of single mothers raising their kids without the benefit of a male role model. To me, this is a delicate situation because until we are sure that we are ready to commit, having a relationship with her children may not be in their best interests. Children who have already been abandoned by their fathers, whether it was by his choice, or death, or geographic distance, can be vulnerable and may be seeking a replacement for that absent male. In the case with my girlfriend, her son's father passed away while we were dating.

What if you begin to form a bond with these children, and then a month later it doesn't work out with the woman? Do you then end the relationship with the children? I have friends who have been involved with single mothers and have admitted that they missed the children as much as the mother when the relationship ended. Did the children deserve the experience of another man disappearing? I've seen the same thing happen with women dating men who have children. I was raised by my father, and I became close to a woman he dated for a number of years. When it ended, I certainly missed her presence.

I've met many women raising two or three children without any help from the fathers. We have to respect these women and, by extension, their children, by not starting a relationship with them when we know that we're not going to be a consistent presence in their lives. At the same time, we can't let the fact that they have children frighten us away. If you think you like a woman and she has children, don't let it stop you from getting to know her, but get to know *her* first. Once the two of you have established your relationship, then and only then is it time to meet the children.

As the child of a divorced couple, I hold this subject very close to my heart. I know how hard it is to see your parents apart, or even to imagine them with new people. You're caught between wanting your parents to be happy and not wanting to see them with someone new. It's no secret that most children pray and hope that their parents will get back together, that one day they will be a family again. But what a lot of children come to learn through this experience is that there is more than one way to be a family. If you manage to create a peaceful and positive dynamic, then everyone benefits, especially the children, who can move from feeling disjointed and fractured to a feeling of stability, support, and structure.

If your partner is divorced with children, he or she will likely remain in regular contact with his or her ex. Their current relationship will have an impact on your relationship. If they're on good terms and have a cordial relationship, then it might not be a challenge to find a way for all of you to coexist harmoniously. If the relationship between your partner and his or her ex is acrimonious, then that will introduce additional challenges to your relationship, if for no other reason than it is a source of stress for your partner.

My friend Georgina was a single mother until she recently remarried. She usually divided the men she met into two groups: the ones who were interested in going out with her but clearly were not ready for a family, and the ones who pursued her precisely *because* they were interested in having a family. She said those men acted as though there was a void in her life that they were there to fill. "But there was no void. My daughter, Val, didn't need a father; she had one. And I wasn't simply in search of any man; I wanted to meet the right man for me."

When Georgina met Frank, the man who would become her new husband and Val's stepfather, he stood out right away because he didn't fit into either of those groups. He treated Georgina as a woman whose affections and trust he'd have to earn. He got to know her on her terms, not on his. He didn't try to walk into their lives and assume the position of man of the house. To Georgina's credit, she didn't act like a mom when they hung. When they went out, they went *out.*

Over the time that Georgina and Frank have been together, his role in their lives has expanded. He has become an authority figure in Val's life, but what cements that relationship is not her fear of his authority but her love and respect for him. She listens to what he says (most of the time) because she knows that he honestly loves her, that he doesn't see her as some add-on that came with her mother.

The relationship between Georgina and her ex-husband was never that good. They fought a lot when they were married, and that didn't change much after they got divorced. There was a lot of animosity, and that proved to be a tough situation for Frank. He decided early on to stay out of it.

After Georgina had an argument with her ex, Frank would listen to her and then ask, "How can we resolve this?" That was usually enough to get her to change gears, so that she moved away from being upset at her ex and toward problem-solving mode.

Parents come to relationships with specific needs and concerns that are different from those of people who are not parents. They have the happiness and well-being of their children to consider, and they have to weigh that before deciding whether to begin dating someone. When is an appropriate time to introduce that someone to their children? When—if at all—should they allow their partner to spend the night while the children are in the house? The list of considerations is long.

Georgina said that sometimes she wouldn't even tell a new man that she had a child until she'd gotten to know him a little better. "It would overwhelm some of them," she told me. "They'd start trying to figure out stuff we weren't even ready for yet, like whether they could envision themselves parenting another man's child, and whether I'd be open to having more children if we were to get married."

While those issues are all worthy of consideration, I agree with Georgina. In the beginning of a relationship, if it doesn't feel right, we don't have to feel pressure to share everything about ourselves. That's what the "getting to know each other" process is all about. After all, in relationships between two child-less people, it would be somewhat off-putting if, on your first date, the person you're out with asked if you could see yourself having children should the two of you end up getting married. It's premature. The fact that a woman or a man has a child from a previous relationship doesn't make such a topic of discussion any less premature or off-putting.

That said, I'm not so sure Georgina's habit of hiding the fact that she's a mother is a good way to begin a relationship. A lie of omission is still a lie. While I understand the reasons behind her decision, it's a huge piece of information to suddenly drop in someone's lap, especially after they've started feeling like they've broken the ice.

If a person doesn't feel comfortable with the fact that you're a parent, then that should tell you something about their readi-ness for the sort of relationship that you need. Waiting before you spring the information is only delaying the inevitable. If your mate can't handle it, then you've wasted your time. If he or she can, and you've waited a long time to reveal this information, he or she might leave anyway, wondering what else you've neglected to mention.

When Nichole told me that she had an adolescent daughter, Jade, it changed the way I thought of her, but not in a negative or detrimental way. My admiration grew; she became more of a woman to me. I have witnessed how difficult it is to be a single parent, and because I volunteer with adolescents, I have some idea of the challenges they go through with their parents. I hap-pen to believe that parenting is one of the most, if not the most, important responsibility someone can have, so I was awed by the fact that she was doing it on her own. My exact thought was: *Wow. Look at this beautiful, smart woman, a math whiz, who is raising a daughter by herself, and she still has the lightness of being.* I wanted to get to know her better.

I realize that some men wouldn't feel that way—which is why you'll find that some older men choose to date women who are much younger. They are more apt to look for women without much of a serious romantic history. But there are a number of men, myself included, who prefer to date women who are closer to our age, women who are more mature and who have had an eventful past, complete with life experience and career accomplishments. If I like someone, I celebrate *everything* about her past. It is *all* of her past experiences—positive and not so positive—that have made her exactly who she is. Change one thing, and she would not be the same person. This holds true even for the men she dated before me. I am not one of those guys that wants to act as if a woman didn't date other guys. As far as I am concerned, if I like her, it's their loss.

14.

Going, Going, Gone: *Crossing the Color Line*

———— ❧ ————

We know all too little about the factors that affect the attitudes of the peoples of the world toward one another. It is clear, however, that color and race are at once the most important and the most enigmatic.

—John Hope Franklin,
married to Aurelia Whittington Franklin for fifty-nine years,
until her death in 1999

It happened during a shoot I was doing for a BET special on the presidential election at the Roosevelt Hotel in Los Angeles. A friend of mine from Harvard was in town, and we made plans to meet at one of my favorite restaurants, Katsuya. After completing the BET shoot, I headed over to the restaurant where I was supposed to meet my friend. As usual, Katsuya was red-carpet busy. While I was waiting, my friend called to say that she was running a half hour late.

I was all alone, with some time to kill, and I noticed three women from the makeup, hair, and wardrobe crew from the shoot earlier in the day having drinks. I made eye contact and waved them over to my table. All three were attractive Black women, ranging in size, age, and hue. One physical trait they did have in common was their smiles, which were wide and welcoming, and as they made their way over to the table, each of them strutted with sexy confidence, as if they owned the place. And I smiled as I watched them walk over, saying to myself, "I *love* Black women." It seemed they had been at the bar and were just finishing their second round. I asked them to join me at my table and offered to buy a third round. "Sushi and sake on me!"

We were laughing and joking and having a great time, when suddenly, two of them stopped laughing. Denise, the pretty, petite caramel brown sister with a pixie do, leaned over to her coworker Andrea, who was a thick-in-all-the-right-places older sistah with light eyes and the kind of skin tone that is often referred to as "redbone." The two of them whispered to each other for a second and then nudged our third table companion. "Keisha ... don't look now, but your ex just walked in. Please keep it cool, girl."

The mood at the table changed in an instant. Keisha, my pleasant-natured new friend with the curly hair and skin that was so dark chocolate it looked almost liquid, suddenly sat up straight. Without turning her head, she asked her coworkers whether her ex was alone. Denise, the petite sister, shook her head.

"Girl," Denise sighed, "no. He has his arms around that fat Latin chick he said was his coworker. Now he is kissing her on the neck!" I sat slightly dumbfounded by the drama that was unfolding before me. Slowly sipping my sake, I carefully asked, "Um ... is everything okay, ladies?"

Boy, was that the wrong question to ask. Suddenly Keisha, who only moments before had been slapping her sexy thighs while laughing at my story, burst into silent tears. I could tell she was upset with her emotional display, because as quickly as tears fell from her wide hazel brown eyes, she tried to wipe them off of her face. "I knew it," she said. "I knew it. I am so tired of this. He always used to tell me that he was getting tired of sisters. Guess at least he told me the truth about one thing."

Now utterly lost, I put my hand on top of hers and said, "Ah, sweetie, don't cry. I know it can't feel good to see your ex with another woman, but hey, from what I can see, it's his loss. Look at you; you're beautiful. The next man will take his place in your heart in no time. I'm sure you already have a line at your door waiting on you to show up."

Man, if these ladies thought I was funny before, their response to my serious statements would have made you think I was the last comedian on earth. They all started laughing, while at the same time shaking their heads no.

"Hill," Andrea said with a slight attitude, "not in L.A. she doesn't!" To which Denise added, "Or Miami, New York, or hell, even Atlanta these days." The two slapped five. I was completely lost. Exasperated, wanting to be let in on the inside scoop, I asked the three ladies, "What are you guys talking about, and what is so funny about what I said? I was just trying to make Keisha feel better."

"Hill," Keisha responded, "take a look around the restaurant. Tell me how I could possibly feel any better at this moment." I looked around. The restaurant looked the same as it did on any other night, and because I ate there regularly, I knew the scene well: sexy people, sexy couples, wearing sexy clothes, eating sexy food, having a sexy time. With the exception of our increasingly depressing table, everyone seemed to be enjoying themselves. Shrugging my shoulders, and then leaning back in my chair, I took a sip of water. "I see people having fun," I said. "Except the three of you, mad at a man who is not even remotely aware of the effect his presence is having on you." I wanted Keisha to realize that any man that left her is actually doing her a favor, that he is unnecessary for her future journey.

Finally, Andrea blurted out, "Ugh! Hill, look at those couples." She pointed at a table with three couples. "What do they have in common?" At the table sat three brothas with three clearly non-Black women; one Asian, one blonde, and one brunette who looked kind of Middle Eastern.

"What? That one table?" I waved them off.

"Not one of them is with a Black woman. You gonna tell me that with all the hot chocolate women in L.A. they couldn't have found at least one who was good enough to sit at their table?" Keisha threw out.

All sorts of retorts swirling in my head, I came back with a response, "I see at least three or four Black couples in this room that you didn't even acknowledge, and . . . what does being good enough have to do with it? You don't even know those guys. They might not be any of your types, but just because they're with White women you think that makes you inferior in their eyes?"

Andrea put up her hand in the stop formation to quell any more of my thoughts. "Yeah, and don't even try to make an excuse about it being just coincidence or something. Hill, this scene is almost the same in every club, lounge, and nice restaurant in every city across the country." To this statement, Keisha slowly nodded, saying, "Yeah, ever since Diddy showed brothas that Latin women have big asses, it's like sisters have been at the bottom of the heap." Then Denise sarcastically added, "Yeah, I even heard the White actress on *The Game* gets more fan mail from brothas than the sistahs on the show." I couldn't tell if she was serious or joking. But no one else laughed.

Feeling slightly shocked at the drastic turn in our conversation, I fumbled around for something to say to these ladies to lift what less than ten minutes before had been extremely jovial spirits.

"So how come you ladies aren't trying 'something new'?" I tried to joke, but they weren't having it. "Come on, ladies," I said, "it can't be that bad!"

It was at this point in the conversation that the hostess arrived with my dinner companion—my old grad school friend. My very tall, very thin, very blonde, very blue-eyed, freckle-faced, excited college friend: Ally.

When Ally arrived at the table, she immediately squealed, her face filled with sheer delight. She scooped me up into a hug from behind and began showering my face and head with friendly kisses. If looks could kill, I assure you, I wouldn't be writing right now. At Ally's jubilant arrival, the table got deadly silent.

Looking from me to Keisha to Denise to Andrea, my naive-to-it-all friend swished her long hair to the side and with a flip of her hand extended it to the lady closest to her, who happened to be Keisha. "Hello there," Ally twanged with her distinct, upper-crust New England accent. "I'm Ally. It's a pleasure." In response to her introduction, the two women farthest from her rose and sauntered back toward the bar, to the same spot where they'd been sitting earlier when I waved them over.

As Keisha slowly stood up and reached for her purse, she looked right at Ally and responded, "Ally, was it? Well, I wish I could say the same, but right now I can't." She then turned to me and stared me dead in the eyes. "Hill," she said, "I thought you were one of the few left. Guess I was wrong." Cutting her eyes, she walked away to rejoin her two friends.

I was stunned. They'd completely misunderstood my situation, but I also suddenly understood them on a level that I hadn't earlier. Keisha's words cut me deeply. Ally flounced into her seat, leaned over close to me, and said, "Sheesh. What was their problem? Talk about attitudes." Then she pushed Keisha's crumpled, tear-stained napkins off the table and onto the floor. She scooted her chair in closer to me and whispered, "So fill me in on everything. Don't you just absolutely love L.A.?"

Seeing my three former drinking companions by themselves at the bar, I wanted to go over and say something to restore their faith. But for a second I thought, hadn't they just dumped their baggage on me without asking me one question about my situation or giving me the benefit of the doubt? And what if I did like this White woman? Would that mean I hated Black women or thought less of them? As I looked back at that conversation, it became clear that these sisters were in many ways using their words, thoughts, and actions to create their beliefs. They quickly let me know how they felt about interracial dating and how it made them feel inferior. They then proceeded to repeat the mantra that in L.A., Black men prefer White women. Sadly, by the end of our conversation, they thought that their beliefs were validated.

Whenever I tell this story, people want to know where I stand on the issue of interracial dating. Is it okay? Well, yes *and* no. On the public level, yes, because I believe that consenting adults should be allowed to feel completely free to fall in love with whomever they fall in love with. Now, on a private level, for me, I personally envision myself married to a Black woman.

It was only forty-two years ago that the Supreme Court (in a case ironically called *Loving v. Virginia*) struck down a Virginia law that banned Whites from marrying non-Whites. Up until that point, interracial dating was illegal in this country. According to the Census Bureau, Black-White marriages went up from 65,000 in 1970 to 422,000 in 2006—an increase of almost 650 percent.

For a long time, odds were that if a couple was interracial, the man was Black and the woman was White, but increasingly that ratio is evening out as more Black women become involved with White men. Popular films like *Jungle Fever*, the story of a relationship between a Black man, played by Wesley Snipes, and a White woman, played by Annabella Sciorra, came out in 1991 when Black men with White women was the dominant trend in interracial dating. But in 2006, *Something New*, a film with my girl Sanaa Lathan and Simon Baker featured a Black woman and a White man in a romantic relationship.

Adjoa, a friend of mine, a dark African sister who grew up in New York, lived for a few years with a White man in Manhattan. She tells the story of being absolutely shocked by the way strangers felt perfectly comfortable trying to insert themselves into her relationship. Adjoa's boyfriend was blond, blue-eyed, tall, and Germanic looking, while she is petite and curvaceous with long, thick dreadlocks. She said Black men and women would freely comment on her relationship in ways that they would never dream of publicly commenting on a relationship between a Black man and a Black woman. Adjoa recalls walking down the street with her boyfriend and hearing two Black folks yell after her, "He's using you, girl! He's using you!" She and her boyfriend have since broken up but have remained very close friends. Now married to a brother from Jamaica, Adjoa said that she had these sorts of experiences on a regular basis all over Manhattan and other cities, but that was years ago.

I have another friend, Kelley, who is Black and recently married a White man, with whom she has two beautiful boys. She and her husband have traveled all over the world without any significant incidents, looks, or rude comments. They seem so well suited and happy that I can only thank God they found each other. It's like my aunt used to say: "If some people didn't go outside their race, they'd be single."

I realize that this is a touchy subject for many of us, and our opinions on these issues may continually evolve. "But what if the interracial dating isn't about love?" a few of my friends have asked. "What if it's about not wanting to be with a Black woman (or man) because of some deeper self-hate issues and insecurities?" Obviously, there are people who make choices for reasons that are less than honorable or authentic. The most we can do to rebuild self-esteem and trust is to continue having conversations with others while concentrating on our shared values, beliefs, and commitments.

I won't discourage anyone from trying "something new." However, I would *encourage* us to not give up on one another. Believe me, there are millions of brothas out there, myself included, who *love* Black women, cherish Black women, and greatly appreciate all the beauty, nurturing, and companionship that our amazing Black women have to offer. And I know there are so many sistahs out there who love and appreciate a kind, considerate brotha of high character. We fit like hand in glove, and when it's right—there's nothing better! It's yet another reason I'm glad Nichole's a part of my life.

SISTERS' SOIREE CHAT II

Hill: Okay, ladies. I have a somewhat sensitive topic I would love to get your thoughts on. Why do you think that Black men date interracially, and how do you feel about it?

Genell: Because Black women are strong-minded and Black men want to have that power over women. They want to control it all. Women of other cultures are taught to be passive. They believe in obeying their men and keeping the man happy, regardless of their own feelings. Black women are too practical to deal with their egos.

Tracy: I think people should date whomever they want as long as they don't discriminate against their own race, but what I do hate is when Black men justify dating Asian and Hispanic chicks by saying they are women of color. They are not women of color; they don't have the same experiences, problems, issues, body type, or anything else. They are the complete opposite of Black women, and they will call you a "nigger" in a minute behind closed doors, too, just like blondie.

Brenda: The usual so-called reason I hear Black men give when they date outside their race is that "Black women are bitter and miserable." But, I wonder, "Why?" I think they are being a little too hard on Black women. They act like Black women are saying, "Please don't send me a decent Black man. I *want* to be miserable." The truth is that a *real* good man, of *any race*, is a rare breed. But Black women *are* statistically at a disadvantage when it comes to finding a suitable mate. Do Black women have issues? Yes. Do all women have issues? Yes. Damn near everyone in their dating years has trouble with the opposite sex, male and female, regardless of their race. I just wish that more Black men would stop making it out to be that Black women are the reason for their own loneliness. Because we didn't get here by ourselves.

Iyana: I think it's for a few different reasons. Black women don't stroke their egos; are too controlling; don't listen with their ears or hearts; and won't let them be the men that they are. Too often, we are too busy calling them punks if they don't do it our way.

Valerie: What I can't understand, though, is why Black women—and so many other people—automatically assume because you date outside your race that it's self-hate. My brother's wife is White, and he's never hated himself, and believe me he went through a lot with my closed-minded family, but he married her because he loves her, not because he hates himself. And I have come to love her because she loves him. That is all that matters to me, that it is for love.

Erica: I will say this about Black men who date interracially: It really bothers me when Black men lump together every group of women who are not White into the same group as Black women. I feel like, if I date a Japanese man, he is just a Japanese man. If I date a Puerto Rican man, he is just a Puerto Rican. I don't ever associate these men as being men of *color*. I don't ever associate them as being equal to a Black man. They are not equal in my eyes. They don't have the same looks, style, attitude, issues, or plights as a Black man. Only Black men delude themselves and justify dating Asians and Latinas by calling them "women of color," and that's an insult. I hate it. These women do not identify with us. In fact, many of these so-called women of color feel as if they are better than Black women. I feel like Black men should be honest and call it for what it is: You date Asians and Latinas because you prefer their attitudes or their long hair. It just upsets me when I hear a man say that he will not date a White woman, that he will only date women of color, as if that makes his preference for a race other than Black better just because they are not White. Whatever—it is still the same in the end as far as I'm concerned; you might as well be dating a White girl.

Sarita: First off, I think the widely accepted generalization that women of other cultures don't give attitudes is a bunch of bull! My stepmother was a first-generation Chinese woman, and man, she would raise hell on my dad and me, both verbally and physically. It seems to me that when a White girl gets mad she is seen as a victim, and when a Latina woman gets mad she is seen as sexy; it's only the sisters, when we express a universal human emotion, who get labeled as having "bad attitudes." It is also important to realize that just because a woman of another culture is dating a Black man, that does not mean that she loves or even respects the Black culture as a whole, or at all for that matter. As far as Black men who date interracially goes, like that Talib Kweli song starts off, "Even your conditioning has been conditioned Brotha." I think Black men date interracially because they have been socialized to value everything other than Black women. But now it is no longer just White women who are placed on pedestals. Now it has evolved to include any woman, of any culture, who is not Black. I think it's pretty sad. Don't get me wrong; if a Black man is dating a woman of another culture for real love, I have no issue with it. But when Black men feel the need to verbally put down Black women as a way of justifying their interracial partners, I become hurt and disgusted by the same old tired story they give with a list of their reasons why. I look around at the few men in my family, and they are all with women of other races. I look around at the men in my circle who are my age, and I see whom they gravitate toward. I have found that this sad phenomenon mostly seems to be true of men in Los Angeles. I would also say that I have learned a few tricks from observing women of other cultures. I was not really raised to cater to a man, but I see how important that aspect seems to be. It seems to come so naturally to them. So I have kind of had to reraise and retrain myself to have that more gender-traditional nurturing spirit as well.

Tami: Honestly, I used to get real "huffy" in the chest when I saw a Black man with a non-Black woman. I had a double standard for a minute; that's the hypocrite in me. I'm big enough to admit it, because I would never get mad at a Black woman being with a White man. But, let the tables turn, and, oh, Lawd. I'm that Black woman you pass rolling her eyes and making a mean comment loud enough for you both to hear. Then I had to stop and ask myself, "If he approached you, would you want to be with that brotha anyways?" I found that probably ninety-eight percent of the time the answer would be not only no, but hell-to-the-no! So, it doesn't bother me like it used to. Finding love is hard for a lot of people. I'm learning that if you happen to find *true* love, not that fake for-show-shit love, with someone outside of your race . . . *go for it!*

Hill: So what have your personal experiences been with interracial dating or social interactions with men of other cultures?

Aishah: I have dated other races. It's always an issue . . . sometimes big, other times small. Most White men I've dated have always had a physical attraction to Black women but don't try to act Black.

Genell: I've only dated Black men, so I have nothing to compare the experience to.

Karrin: I'm not going to discount anyone because of the color of their skin. I mostly date Black men and have been approached by White men. I wasn't interested in them specifically, but hey, if they step to me, then let's see what happens. I would date a White man or any other ethnicity for that matter. If I find that this person is attractive, has a good head on his shoulders, and treats me well, then common sense would say that you should be all for it, right? I did go out with a White boy for a short period of time when I was younger, and it was very weird at first. But he treated me like a total princess, which sad to say is a lot more than I can say for some of these Black "men" out here today.

Iyana: I've never dated interracially.

Sarita: I've never dated anything other than Black men. But one of my good friends is a White guy who has a strong preference for Black women. I distinctly remember that one of our early conversations was him praising the beauty of Black women. At twenty-six years old, it was the first time in my entire life I had personally heard any man describe a woman who looked like me—a nonexotic, non-mixed-appearing

Black female—as beautiful. And while it made me feel closer and appreciative of him, it also made me sad. Sad that these words fell on my ears for the first time delivered from a White male instead of a Black man. Not my father, not my uncle, not the many men I had dated, not one, until this random White guy. And I shared a quick meal that led to a lifetime of friendship as a result.

Brenda: This surprises people when I admit this, because many consider me as very pretty, but I had the same experiences as Sarita. I'm from Chicago, and when I was coming up, if you were not fair toned or didn't have good hair, you were not hot according to the Black males. Not making a generalization about *all,* but this is what I had been told, to my face, numerous times, to the point where my self-esteem was down to zero at one point when I was little and a young woman. This was not just by strangers, or men either, but also by my family. The exception to this came only when I started dating White men. Everything I had been taught was ugly, they seemed to love. So to this day, I pretty much exclusively date White men. Although Black men approach me now, I don't think I will ever feel comfortable with the idea that they want me in the way that I was raised to want them. Sorry, brothas; this sistah has long moved on.

Stephanie: If you fall in love with someone outside of your race and it is true and makes you happy, then fuck everyone else. I personally have dated all types of men, like roll call at the UN. Men are men and have their share of problems, but the fetishists, who *only* want to date me because I am a Black woman, need to steer clear because it becomes obvious early. That being said, I am pretty damn sure that there are plenty of angry White women sitting alone at home tonight as well. I agree with Brenda when she said that our dating pool is much smaller. I have two master's degrees and am a professional; I refuse to date some dude with bad credit, no education, lives at his mother's house, with no aspirations—*no matter what color he is*!

Tami: I love Black men, and I will marry one, someday, and have his beautiful Black children. There's no doubt in my mind. I am claiming it!

Valerie: Everybody can't have Mr. Tall-Handsome-Successful-Black-Man. It just ain't enough of them to go around. And I don't have a share mentality. So, I shouldn't have to carry the burden of "sticking with my community," walking around conflicted about who I date while the next Black man doesn't care. That's a waste of a life.

Karla: I have only dated Black men, and I don't feel like I'm carrying a burden because of my choice. I don't date Black men because I feel I gotta "stick with my community." I also don't choose who I date based on what other Black men are doing. I'm simply pretty much solely attracted to Black men. Ideally, I want to have a Black husband and build a strong Black family with him, but if I wanted to date a White man, I would and my family would still accept me. I just never made that choice. Even if I decide to make that choice, there are some things that I talk about among other Black people that I'd *never* feel comfortable sharing with a White person. If I shared it, I would not be certain if they'd *truly* understand anyway. How can I build with a person (long term) if

I can never feel truly comfortable being myself and sharing *all* the things that are important to me? That is why I say that I can never really have a serious relationship with a non-Black person (particularly a White one). Although I am twenty-eight and not married, I don't feel like my life is wasted. The numbers are not in my favor, but I believe that there are still some decent brothers around. I have a good one now, and if he acts up, I've got some cuties on the bench waiting to get in the game. I just know that if I was seen with a White husband, it would probably be because I'm settling, and I don't settle.

Sonya: Black men don't seem to think twice or feel conflicted about dating interracially, so why should I? I am tired of waiting for the ever-elusive "right Black man," and I don't want to waste my time worried about someone who isn't worried about me. On a personal level, I honestly would rather marry a Black man, but where I live, the odds are just not in my favor. I'm giving moving to another city, like maybe Washington, D.C., a shot, but in the meantime, I'm going to work on getting over my sense of obligation to a group of men that doesn't share feelings of obligation to me. There are men out there who have the "Nubian nuisance" mentality, and I can't waste time losing sleep over it. I need to be out doing what's good for me, too.

Nikki: I date any man who seems like he will be fun and good to me. It doesn't matter if he is Black, White, Asian, or Puerto Rican. The problem I have with dating interracially actually comes more from other sistahs who are so quick to jump in my private business and wave the "you shouldn't date nothing but a Black man" banner. The irony of it all is that many of these women tend to lean toward being the angry, miserable, and alone stereotype placed upon Black women. So because it seems like they have been too conditioned to consider dating any man other than a Black man, they try to make other Black women miserable too by trying to guilt them out of interracial dating, in order to keep them in the "I'm single and mad about it because I won't date nothing but a Black man" box, too. No, thank you. I will take happiness in whatever form it is presented to me.

Trace: Fuck being politically correct. If I am attracted to a *man* of any race, and we are compatible, then we are dating. It is real simple, people; if you don't wanna date other races, *don't*. If you do wanna date other races, go ahead and fucking do!

Erica: I will most likely *never* date outside my race. Even though I live in a state which is only two percent Black, and damn near *all* the brothas here date White women, I'm one of those Black women who will be by my damn self before I date a White man. To me, there just isn't anything more beautiful than a dark, well-defined, muscular Black man. I will be honest; I have kissed a White man before, and it just felt so wrong. So just the thought of screwing one makes me wanna hurl. And in my humble personal opinion, those brothas who marry, date, and mass produce with those blondes have serious *self-hate* issues going on, and it's just sad!

Dana: Me, personally, I do not care about the color of a man. You can be Black, White, purple, green, brown, orange, red, blue, or yellow for all I care; as long as you have a nice personality it can be all good. If it were not for a Black man and a White woman deciding to get married and have children a few generations ago, I probably would not exist. And I wish my family would act all saddity for me dating outside my race, because I will promptly put them in check and remind them of their heritage in a heartbeat.

BLACK MEN SPEAK IV

Hill: All right, brothas. What have your dating experiences or social interactions with women of other cultures been?

Brad: This doesn't apply to me. I have not dated, and do not date, interracially. The reason being, I just believe in being the positive side of statistics of Black men in America. I don't want to be another Black man who took his "good attributes" elsewhere. I would rather keep it in-house and build more Black success stories for the next generation.

Chris: I dated interracially in my younger days, but for me, it simply became something I was not comfortable with. There are things that just *are* regarding interracial relationships, and with all the other challenges in relationships, why bring in one that you truly have no control over?

Jared: My philosophy is, "If it ain't White, then it's all right!" Black men should not be ostracized for dating Latino, Arab, or Asian women. They go through the same thing we go through and understand us. And many times, they treat us better than sistahs!

Kev: I actually put White women in a different category from women of color. Ultimately, I look at the principle and the future of things. Even as a young cat, I could never see myself coming home to my living room and there being a picture on the wall of, like, me, and my wife being a White woman, with a bunch of mixed kids. I could never see that for myself. So if I can't see that, I really can't go there. So I never really had interest in seeing what it would be like dating a White woman.

Eric: When you see a brotha walking down the street with a White girl on his arm, you automatically think that one of them is rich. Either he made it and got himself a White girl to up his status, or she was a rich White girl, looking for a little Black loving in the bed to keep her right. It is usually one of those two things. Heck, there are places that are famous for rich White women looking for brothas to take care of. I heard that Santa Barbara in California is one of them.

Johnny: Oh, here we go. Black women are rallying up for their favorite "let's bash the Black men" theme. You know how it goes: Black men say we are ugly; Black men are with non-Black women; oh, God, *the Black man is the worst thing walking this earth*. The truth is that most Black men love Black women. Statistically, most Black men are with Black women. Who people choose to date is their business, and this bashing Black men is really tired. The truth is that some Black women are just as fucked up as the Black men they are bashing. I can see why so many of them are having so many lonely nights. They need to stop worrying themselves to death about the Black men that sure ain't worrying about them, and focus some positive attention on the brothas who are.

Warren: For some of us the slave gene is real. That is what 450-plus years of depression and oppression has done to Black folks. Ultimately, I believe that you love who you love. But some of us, as I said, have that slave gene working overtime. Now as for myself, I love Black women. But I would date a Spanish chick or an Asian chick as well. I would like to marry a Black woman. But as long as she is of color, that is what matters the most. I can't date a White chick because I just don't find them attractive. Plus, White women age badly as they get older. That is a turnoff in my book.

Hill: So, in general, would you say there are differences?

Brad: Again, never done it, so wouldn't know.

Chris: I would say yes there are, but again I think that varies from person to person. I don't hate on those who feel one way or the other. This is just me and my thoughts. The differences are not that significant like some men would like to have you believe. At the end of the day, women are women.

Jared: White women, for the most part in my experience, have higher libidos than all other races.

Dietrich: There are some differences. There are some similarities. I've dated Asian women, who on the surface are a lot more docile. Latinas are really family oriented. And it's crazy because most of the Latinas that I've dated don't want to date Latin guys because of the way they treat their women. So that culture is also experiencing this. Except they seem to be going more toward the stereotypical all-American White guys. They are looking to interracially date a man that is going to socially pull them up. White women, in my experience, are a lot flakier, for lack of a better term.

Kev: It takes a whole lot more for a sistah to pour into you what women of other cultures do automatically because of their upbringings and lack of trust issues. Most of us who are under the age of thirty-five and are Black seem to have come up without fathers in our homes. Well, that's not the case for most White women and women of other cultures. Usually they come up with both parents in the home in some capacity. So the reason why it is so-called easier to date White women, or women who are not Black, is because they automatically do not have a trusting issue. Many sistahs have been played. She gave her body to a dude and he treated her like nothing. So she is either introverted, or she makes a point to put up a wall that is almost impossible to get through. So automatically, the stage is set up for complete failure. She is on some, "Where were you? Why didn't you call me back? You ain't no good, just like Ricky, Jerome, and Bobby." Whereas, when I have dated, like, Latina chicks, there wasn't any of that, and we were in two different places at two different times. When we were together, it was all about me to the point of where I felt I had to reciprocate. She would cook me dinner, she would take care of me, and she would want to do the dishes! It got to be where I would be, like, "No, baby, you sit down, and let me take care of you." Because if I am a good guy, and I get treated like that? I want to give that back, and massage your feet, and run your bubble bath. All that positivity you pour into me, I want to give back to you. So sistahs need to realize this is a very true factor in men deciding to date women who are not Black. Whether they want to agree with it or not, it is the reality of it.

PART 4:
PULLING UP THE ROOTS

❦

FROM THE DESK OF HILL HARPER

12/16

- I'm still afraid, but I know that

    FEAR = FALSE EVIDENCE
              APPEARING REAL

- I definitely thought I'd be married with kids by now.

- Is she out with other guys? Am I as good a lover as other dudes she has been with? Why am I feeling insecure right now?

- I know that people who are married are more successful. And I have big goals and dreams. But why does that fear voice say that settling down will take me away from what I want to accomplish?

    <Long distance is tough. The time apart feels like forever.>

❦

15.

E-Race-ing the Rules

Here's to the crazy ones . . . who see things differently—they're not fond of rules. . . . You can quote them, disagree with them, glorify or vilify them, but the only thing you can't do is ignore them because they change things . . . they push the human race forward.

Steve Jobs,
married to Laurene Powell since 1991

What exactly are the rules of dating and relationships? I'm not sure I even know. I used to when I was younger, in high school. Back then, dating was an activity, a sport that we talked about, dissected, and your dating prowess was even rated. Oh, I knew what every hand gesture, smile, laugh, wink, nod, and comment meant, suggested, or implied. I knew that if a girl crossed her legs when we started kissing, that meant she would more than likely uncross them later in the evening. I knew that the girls who unbuttoned their blouses halfway down without even being asked would never let you see an inch more of flesh than that, no matter how hard you tried or how nicely you asked.

But high school was ages ago. I'm no longer a football player using my dad's car on a Friday night. I'm a grown man hoping to meet and connect with a woman with whom I can share my life. Each time I go out on a first date with a woman, it's like cracking open the cover of a new journal and seeing that blank page. The possibilities are endless. I observe as much as I can about the woman's movements and gestures. I try to listen not only to what she's saying but also to what she's trying to tell me. But I don't turn it into a game full of rules and restrictions, like we did when I was in high school.

I have to say that sometimes I don't feel the same is true of the women I date. Sometimes it feels as though they're trying to apply some of those old, outdated high school rules we used to follow back then—not to the date, but to all the things that happen afterward. How soon do I call? What do I say when I call? How long does it take for me to ask her on a second date? Even when I try to explain myself, I always feel as though I've broken a rule and that act of insolence has badly offended her.

Let me try to be more specific. Last year, I went out on a date with a lovely woman who painted the most spectacular artwork. We sat at the restaurant and talked and talked and talked until we realized that we were the last customers there. The staff was waiting on us so they could clean off our table, close the place, and go home to their families. It was a perfect date.

I couldn't stop thinking about her the next day. If I'd had my way, I would have called her and asked her to have dinner with me that night, too. But I was working. I had a very early call time and it ended up being an eighteen-hour day. By the time I got home, I was spent and I didn't want to call her so late. Based on the comments I'd heard my female friends make, I knew that women don't think too highly of men who call at very late hours. I didn't want her to think I was making a booty call. So I put off calling her until the next day.

Just my luck! The next day ended up being as long as the day before. Every spare moment I had, I was trying to memorize my lines. Again, by the time I got home, it was much too late to call. In hindsight, I realize that I probably should have sent her a text or an e-mail, but I felt that was rude and not especially representative of the type of connection we'd shared at dinner. But I guess it would have been better than nothing at all.

By the time I called her the next day, it was obvious she was already through with me. "I'd been hoping to hear from you sooner," she said. I was a bit taken aback. I hadn't expected her to put me on the spot like that. I explained that my work schedule had been crazy. "Uh-huh," she groaned, letting me know that she was not buying it. "Must be hard to get things done when you have to work eighteen-hour days back-to-back like that and you can't even make *any* phone calls."

I was shocked. What could I say? I felt cornered, and that made me angry, so I just wished her a good day and got off the phone without even attempting to ask her out again. I didn't understand why she had to bust my chops like that. My not calling soon enough for her liking didn't mean that I wasn't interested in her, let alone that I was disrespecting her. It only meant that I chose not to call her from a busy set in between takes, or to send her a text message saying something ridiculous like *nice c-ing u. want 2 go 4 dinner l8r 2nite?* I mean, c'mon. How juvenile would that have seemed? So why did I suddenly find myself staring at my phone, feeling like a pimply-faced adolescent who'd just been read by a girl in front of the lockers during a free period?

What a lot of women have to understand is that not all men are trying to tell crafty lies. Sometimes when a man says that he is in meeting and he'll have to call you back, it's possible that he really is in a meeting, and he really does intend to call you back. What's so wrong with giving a man the benefit of the doubt?

Men are very different creatures from women. We don't communicate the same way. We are simple. If you pay attention, you don't have to try to figure out what we mean. We tell you exactly what we mean even when you don't want to hear what we are saying. For instance, when a man says, "I'm not ready to be in a relationship," what he means is, "I'm not interested in being in a serious relationship." Unfortunately, many of my friends take this as a challenge and work to change a man's mind. He's not going to change his mind.

If you are having a great time and enjoying the relationship, why does it need to end up in marriage? Every man you date is not the one you should marry. Some relationships help you grow in different ways. Take a trip down relationship memory lane. Aren't there people you enjoyed dating but are glad you didn't marry? There is a lot to be learned in these transitional pairings, but instead of enjoying all the gifts a relationship has to offer, many of my female friends get resentful. They get angry and blame the man for wasting their time . . . because clearly his time wasn't important, and a relationship that was a two-way street becomes a one-lane road that led to him taking advantage of you. Here is why that is not the truth. He told you exactly what the deal was in the beginning, and yet, you stayed. When you didn't get your needs met, you pointed the finger of blame at him instead of looking in the mirror. When he said he didn't want to be in a relationship or wasn't ready to be in a relationship, that was your cue to keep it moving if you were looking for happily ever after.

In the mid-nineties, there was a book about relationships that was all the rage with women. It was called *The Rules: Time-Tested Secrets to Capturing the Heart of Mr. Right*. All of my female friends read it and were quoting from it, telling me things like, "Can you believe he called me on Wednesday and asked me to go out with him on Friday? I've been dying to go to that Sade concert, too, but I had to tell him no because it's against the rules." After weeks of hearing how one thing or another was against the rules, I finally broke down and demanded to know whose rules these were because they sounded completely ridiculous to me. The book was written by Ellen Fein and Sherrie Schneider, two married women who apparently had learned a bit of age-old wisdom about snagging a husband from a friend who'd learned it from her grandmother.

The Rules was essentially a guide book to how to act on a date (smile a lot and don't talk about yourself), when to turn down dates (if they are made less than four days in advance), and when to sleep with a man (never on the first date). I just couldn't understand it. I mean, really. Do you need to follow directions on how to arrange a date with a man? And as far as not saying yes to last-minute requests: What about spontaneity? What about being a free spirit? Aren't there men who like that and want to marry women who have those traits and tendencies?

As for sex on a first date, I know quite a few couples—married couples—who had sex on their first date, and that didn't stop the men from asking the women to don white dresses and say "I do." I guess my point is that we tend to overanalyze what should or shouldn't be done in a relationship or in

> ❧
> Be sincere when it comes to apologies and explanations.
> ❧

a new dating situation. Everyone is different, and not all actions will have the same intention or translate into the same thing. We simply need to trust our instincts. If something doesn't feel right to you, or if you don't feel like a man is treating you respectfully, then by all means kick him to the curb. But before you do, make sure you're not relying on someone else's interpretation of his actions. Trust your own rules of self-respect and decent behavior. Be sincere when it comes to apologies and explanations.

Part of the wonder and possibility of a first date is that we get to write our own rules, make our own mark on that crisp white sheet of paper in the journal. We get to write our own book on how to be together.

Another thing that's turning relationships topsy-turvy and getting folks all mixed up is gender roles and expectations. In some cases the traditional roles no longer apply, but in others they're still in use. It's hard to know which is which and where you fit in. Messages are mixed up, misconstrued, or just not properly communicated. Earlier, when I mentioned that a man wants a woman he can provide for and protect, some women might have read that as me suggesting that a man wants a woman who will let him be the breadwinner, while she is the homemaker. As I explained, though, a man can provide for a woman in all kinds of ways, up to and including staying home with the kids while she works outside the home. For example, if a woman says she wants a man who is financially responsible, men might read that as her wanting a man who will take care of her financially, when in fact she is saying she wants a man who pays his bills and is not in debt. It is strange territory

> ❧
>
> Don't be afraid to step outside of the box.
>
> ❧

we find ourselves in—not yet fully divorced from the past, and not yet married to new definitions of these terms and these roles. So what to do? How can we avoid getting stuck in the confusion of it all?

I suppose the simplest answer would be to continue having the conversation. It's an opportunity to iron out the kinks that keep us from understanding each other. It's important for us to present to each other our vision of ourselves, including the roles that we choose to occupy in our lives and in our homes.

Just as our culture is changing, our notion of relationships is changing. If Black men and Black women are going to continue moving forward together, then we're going to have to start defining and redefining what the Black family is and is not. The days of us being relegated to a monolithic representation are long over. Black relationships and Black families come in all stripes and have all combinations of gender roles, duties, and responsibilities.

There are Black men who are the primary caretakers of the children and women who are the eighteen-hour-day executives; there are two-person work-at-home families, bicoastal families—you name it. So don't be afraid to step outside of the box. Put aside other people's rules. They don't always work for us, and in the end, they might just make us miss out on what could have been a wonderful situation.

16.

Mad Money

─────────── ❧ ───────────

Money, as it turned out, was exactly like sex. You thought of nothing else if you didn't have it and thought of other things if you did.

James Baldwin,
an American novelist, writer, playwright, poet, essayist, and
civil rights activist, whose work dealt with racial and
sexual issues in the mid-twentieth century

I was recently on an empowerment speaking tour around the country to historically Black colleges and universities. Brilliant and enthusiastic students would show up at every stop, but I noticed two things that truly scared me: first, the lack of financial literacy that had been imparted to these young people by our generation, and second, the huge disparity in the female-to-male student ratio. On one campus there were eleven female students to every one male (and this was a coed institution). On the plane ride home, I started to wonder, Are these two things related? Has our community's lack of cross-generational wealth building had an effect on other aspects of our community? The quality of schools? The incentives for young males to make so-called quick money and not get an education? Is it possible that we can we trace our severe problems with sustaining healthy Black female-male relationships directly to our lack of financial literacy?

When couples are asked what they argue about, in nearly every survey, the answer is money. As a group, Blacks are the largest debtors in the world. Living with debt hanging over our heads causes stress. That stress affects our moods, our quality of life, and our ability to connect with others. The pressure debt creates is not very different from that created by a chronic stomach ache or indigestion. The pain limits our choices and impacts our relationships. Biggie had a song, "Mo' Money, Mo' Problems," but our lives shouldn't be that way. We as a people have in*debt*gestion even though we are earning more money than we ever have before. Part of the problem is that we are running through our credit at alarming rates, and the resulting debt is affecting our relationships. This in*debt*gestion may be the true cause of why the Black family is ill.

Blacks spend more of every dollar we earn than any other ethnic group. Collectively, we carry more than $200 billion in credit card debt alone. Issues of debt, financial stability, and employment have always been stressors in our community. Few other ethnicities have had the challenge of raising as many generations on the meager resources that have been available to us.

Money is a big issue in the life of any romantic partnership, and it's not surprising that there are problems creating financial cohesion in the relationships of Black women and men. These problems manifest in various ways. Let's begin with the biggest problem—how money keeps us apart—because we can't heal whatever's hurting us if there is no us.

Newsweek recently reported that Black women outnumber Black men—24 percent to 17 percent—in the professional-managerial class. The Journal of Blacks in Higher Education, citing Department of Education statistics, reported that Black women earn 67 percent of all bachelor's degrees that are awarded to Blacks, as well as 71 percent of all master's degrees, and 65 percent of all doctoral degrees. According to the 2006 U.S. Census, the more education and money a Black woman has, the less likely she is to marry and have children. What!?!

The numbers are fascinating and shocking, but most of us were already aware of these truths. They're common knowledge; so common, in fact, that they've found their way into the dialogues of many television shows and movies that concern themselves with the lives of single Black women. I hear time and time again from my Black female friends that there is a shortage of "good" men out there, and almost always, "good" is subconsciously linked to earning power.

"I don't care how much potential a man has," my friend Mary told me. "I'm not working to put him through school so that he can leave me the minute he's done. I watched my mama and her girlfriends play that story out. That's not gonna be me."

Plenty of Black women have taken on the role of sole breadwinner, in addition to being homemaker, in order to allow their husbands the freedom to pursue a higher degree. In

> Seventy percent of professional Black women are unmarried.

some instances, once those men had achieved their educational and

professional goals, they dumped the women who'd made those sacrifices for them. Now, I think it's also important to acknowledge that
there are many stories like this that don't end with the women being
wronged. A lot of men, armed with more education and a better
earning potential, stay with the women who supported and believed
in them. Together, the couples meet the goals they set for themselves
and their children.

Only you can decide what sacrifices you should make for a relationship, but some smart sac-
rifices must be made. Don't
believe me? Let me quote you
another statistic: according to
The New York Times, 70 percent
of professional Black women

> ～✤～
> Kindness is one of life's
> most important attributes.
> ～✤～

are unmarried. Now, I am not putting the blame or the responsibility solely on Black women, or discouraging anyone from going for
the best job he or she can get. And when I say that some smart
sacrifices must be made, I mean by Black men as well. We have to
step up and man up. Too many of us are underachieving, but I
believe that will end if we help uplift one another. If you envision your life a certain way, do whatever it takes to turn that vision
into a reality. The same goes for your community. All of us—men
and women—have to move away from thinking that money is
what defines us.

There is a huge difference between self-worth and net worth.
Your self-worth—your potential—has nothing to do with what's
in your pocket. It has to do with *character*: what's in your heart,
how you negotiate your personal relationships, what you place
value on, and how kind you are. (I believe kindness is one of
life's most important attributes.) Net worth is just numbers, just a

bunch of paper. If we confuse that with self-worth, we will find ourselves making poor choices.

In my two previous books, I wrote about financial literacy and the need to solve the debt crisis in our communities. The "debt rule" (only two areas of acceptable debt: property investment and education) and my "new cool money rule" (a wealth building philosophy based around the idea that not every dollar is equal—there is less expensive income/money and costly income/money) are the cornerstones of my thoughts on cross-generational wealth building in the Black community. I believe it is important for men and women—specifically Black men and women—to have frank discussions with each other when it comes to finances and the management of money.

I don't believe in debt. I don't think it's a good idea, and as I've said in other books and lectures, I think the biggest leap forward we can make as a community is to learn to define our self-worth spiritually. Here is a brilliantly insightful quote from Will Smith that I included in my first book, *Letters to a Young Brother*: "Too many people spend money they haven't earned to buy things they don't want, to impress people they don't like." I'm not gonna lie—sometimes buying stuff does feel good in the short term. But too often what we're really buying is debt, and trading away the freedom we could enjoy in the future. When

> ❧
> Share a vision of money goals.
> ❧

put this way, debt accumulation kind of sounds the same as cheating on a partner, and may also require the same level of discipline.

It is true that many of us grew up feeling that we never

had what we needed, or that we didn't have enough. It can easily become a vicious cycle if we don't recognize this. When a person with unresolved feelings about money is suddenly in a two-income relationship, it can feel like he or she finally has some real money to play with. Lots of folks have been waiting a lifetime for that feeling of financial security, so they can kick up their heels and start spending. This can be a recipe for disaster in an otherwise healthy relationship.

Studies show that someone who loves to spend money often finds a partner who prefers to save and is uncomfortable with debt. Obviously this difference will bring conflict into a relationship. It doesn't mean the relationship can't work, but you must talk about money when you get together with another person. It is really important that the two of you have the same goals for the money you make, and the same understanding of what those goals are worth. You don't want the way you spend money to separate you. If money is going to unite you, you need to share a vision of what you are building together and how you want your money to work for you.

Let's say you get involved with someone who is coming into the relationship with mountains of debt. You can, without judgment, help that person learn how to better manage his or her finances or negotiate a payment plan on outstanding balances, provided, of course, the person is ready and willing to change the habits that got him or her there to begin with. Also, it would be wise to wait until the individual has cleaned up his or her credit profile before taking your relationship to the next level. Otherwise, you might end up legally inheriting all that debt as your own. That is no foundation to build a relationship on.

We should talk about our finances not only with our partners but also with our family members. Our ability to build wealth depends on our ability to communicate and create productive habits around money. Talking honestly about your finances with your boyfriend or girlfriend is a necessity if you want to have a strong and long-lasting relationship.

Am I saying that if all of a sudden we eliminated all Black credit card debt, or received reparations or simply our "forty acres and a mule," we would immediately solve the deep-rooted problems we see in Black male-female relationships? Of course not. Money and financial literacy will not solve all the problems, but money is a foundational element of our problems and it is rarely discussed in a broad, relationship-community context. It needs to be a key part of the conversation.

Sharon Epperson, a sister on CNBC, has written *The Big Payoff: 8 Steps Couples Can Take to Make the Most of Their Money— and Live Richly Ever After*. In her book, she offers excellent advice, tackling head-on the financial problems that can poison relationships. I particularly love her "Budget Commandments," three simple rules that both individuals in a relationship can agree to follow:

1. *Thou Shalt Pay Thine Own Self First*. Save and invest a set amount each pay period.
2. *Thou Shalt Stay Out of Debt*. Don't use credit cards to buy things you should pay cash for. Pay credit card bills off in full each month. The National Foundation for Credit Counseling can help.
3. *Thou Shalt Live on One Income, Not Two*. If both of you are working, try to save and invest one paycheck. Yes, you can do it!

I think it's time we look inward to learn what our economic values are. If we find someone we like who doesn't necessarily share our social, spiritual, community, or economic values, we should *encourage* them instead of writing them off. We should seek to inspire them to "get on the bus" with us. Our destination is unreasonable happiness with a quick stopover in wealth city.

17.

Anger, Forgiveness, and Learning to Let Go

Anger is a manifestation of a deeper issue . . . and that, for me, is based on insecurity, self-esteem, and loneliness.

Naomi Campbell,
London-born supermodel and actress, single

Going from one relationship to the next is a lot like moving from one place to another. When you're packing, you have to go through all of your stuff to see what you want to carry with you to the new place. You will recognize that some things, while useful for the place where you once were, will not serve any purpose in the new place, and you need to let them go. That's how it should be with the emotions we amass in relationships. When we see that something will not serve us in a future relationship, we should just let it go.

Take anger, one of the most destructive human emotions if not properly dealt with. My friend Georgina once told me about an experience she had with the FedEx man. Georgina is a clothing designer who works out of her home office. Every afternoon the same FedEx man would come to her door to pick up her packages. They would chat briefly about the weather or something equally harmless. Sometimes he would come late, but since she worked from her home and didn't have to leave, it never really bothered her.

Then one day, he showed up an hour late. Georgina wasn't in a particularly good mood that day. She'd broken up with her then-husband and was raising a child all by herself. Her parents—especially her father—seemed to be siding with her ex and chastising her for allowing the marriage to break up and for not working hard enough to make the marriage last. When the FedEx man arrived at Georgina's door, she started yelling at him.

"I'm sick and tired of you not prioritizing me. All I do is wait and wait and wait for you. What? You think I don't have any plans and goals of my own? I'm tired of you treating me like this. Do you understand?" After she'd finished her diatribe, she looked up at the FedEx man, who was staring at her, stunned. Georgina felt a little embarrassed, but only a little.

"That wasn't about you," she told him. "It was really about my dad, and my mom . . . and my ex-husband. I was mad at them." He said, "Oh," took her package, and left. Even though she'd explained that she hadn't meant to yell at him, the FedEx man never showed up late to pick up her packages again.

If we don't address our anger or direct it to the person who caused it, we usually transfer it onto someone else: someone who is treating us in a way that reminds us of how we were treated that made us angry, or someone who has not treated us badly at all. That's why it is important for us to recognize what the root cause of our anger is.

> Lose the anger.

Maybe you grew up with a father who was controlling. You know that doesn't mean that all men are controlling. Still, you keep your guard up and behave in a way that lets the men in your life know that you're just not having it, that they will not and cannot control you. Maybe your mother was critical of you, but that doesn't mean all women will be critical. Still, you keep your guard up and put every woman in your life on notice: you will not and cannot tolerate their criticism, even to the point that you take compliments as criticism and lash out as a result.

These are common situations. We often carry our baggage from childhood into our relationships. It doesn't even have to be something that's been done to you. It could be something that you've witnessed, like the way that your parents related. If your parents constantly bickered, yelled, and cussed each other out, then living in a hostile environment may feel natural to you, like home. That doesn't mean you want to duplicate it, but we frequently repeat old patterns even if we don't intend to.

> We often carry our baggage from childhood into our relationships.

I'm sure you've heard the saying "Insanity is doing the same thing over and over and expecting different results." Carrying the same baggage from partner to partner and not recognizing how it negatively impacts our relationships is a form of insanity.

Let's commit to learning how to let go of anger and leave it behind so that we don't infect our future relationships. We can do the work it takes to find that root cause and deal with it. People don't like being yelled at for nothing at all. Nor does anyone like being treated with suspicion or over the top jealousy. They don't like being accused of a crime they haven't committed. It's a form of abuse. People who crave healthy and, yes, sane partnerships will not stick around in an abusive situation.

What if your way of responding to past hurts is not by being aggressive but being passive? Instead of expressing anger, you internalize your feelings, soaking them all into your psyche. You become timid and full of self-doubt. You're afraid to speak up and defend yourself.

People who find themselves in this situation are often susceptible to abuse. There are many cases of physically abusive relationships and marriages in the media, but abuse doesn't usually begin that way. Most people would not go out a second time with a man or woman who beat them up on the first date. Abuse begins slowly. It escalates.

I had a friend who told me that her father always told her that she dressed like a slut. He would call her dumb or stupid at least a dozen times every day, telling her that she couldn't do anything right. Is it any wonder, then, that years later she ended up with an abusive husband?

Remember that old kids' rhyme about sticks and stones? Well, words do hurt, and the wounds they create probably take longer to heal than physical wounds. Blocking out the negative effects of words like that, especially if they are incessant, is far easier said than done. It's like a drop of water hitting the surface of a stone. One drop will do nothing, but if the drops keep coming one after the other, they will eventually make an indentation on the surface of that stone. They will leave their mark. Many people who grow up with this type of abuse find themselves repeating the pattern of abuse in their romantic relationships. Once again, they are the victims.

The image we have of women and men who suffer from domestic abuse is extremely misleading. We think of them as timid, fragile, soft-spoken. In actuality, a fair percentage of men and women who find themselves in such situations are over-achievers, people who look amazingly successful and confident on paper. But if you look past the credentials and fancy titles, you find a person with low self-esteem, a person who deep down believes—no matter how hard he or she has worked to disprove it—that there must be some truth in all the negative things that have been said to him or her.

Another form of abuse that I think I should mention in these pages is sexual abuse. Statistics show that at least one in four women experiences some form of sexual abuse in her lifetime. A couple of the women I've been involved with have been survivors of sexual abuse, so I know firsthand that the effects of this sort of abuse linger for years afterward. I've seen that it usually impacts them in one of two ways: either they are extremely guarded with their sexuality or they are overtly sexual and appear to have no boundaries with their bodies.

> ᨊ
> Time is not an enemy but a friend.
> ᨊ

Women carry the hurt in various ways. For some women, it's excess weight gain. For others, it's disconnecting while having sex with a partner. For another group, it's sexual promiscuity, or dressing and behaving in ways that are sexually inappropriate. Letting go of such baggage is not easy. From my own experiences dating women who were sexually abused, I learned that no amount of counseling is too much. I've known people who feel as though they should have recovered from the trauma, that enough time has passed, and that something must be wrong with them. That's not the case. We all heal in our own time—emotionally and physically. Time is not an enemy but a friend.

Something that we forget all too often is that men are also victims of sexual abuse—and that it can also affect their personal relationships and their sense of identity and self-worth. Since men are less apt to report sexual abuse, or discuss it with their friends, the figures are not reliable and vary greatly. Whether you're a man or a woman survivor of sexual abuse, one thing is true: You must deal with it directly in order to heal, and you must be an active participant in your own healing process. In order for you to let go of the rage, fear, and hurt enough that you can develop healthy relationships, you must talk to someone. Remember, a therapist or counselor can also help you figure out how to talk to your partner.

Once, when I was dating a woman who had been sexually abused, I found I had to remind her that most men I know don't enjoy having sex with a partner who is unfulfilled. Sex is supposed to be a shared experience. I want my partner to be happy, satisfied, and healthy. I want our sexual intimacy to be an extension of our emotional intimacy. Most men and women feel this way. That's another reason why it's so vital to have open and honest communication that personifies two people working *together* to move toward a healthy union.

All of the forms of abuse that I've mentioned so far lay the groundwork for discussing physical abuse. People who have been victims of verbal or sexual abuse are much more likely to find themselves in physically abusive relationships. Why is that? Because their self-worth has been shattered.

There is never an excuse that can justify someone hitting his or her partner. No woman or man deserves to be beaten up, slapped, kicked, punched, grabbed, or thrown around. It's unimaginable to me that someone can do something like that to a person they claim to love. Just like cheating, abuse is based on lies. Abusers lie to themselves in order to feel as though they are in the right. They lie in order to beg their victims for forgiveness. They lie in order to cover up the damage that they have done. Once the lies start unraveling, they can be seen for the cowards they really are, but until then, they prey on their victims' fear. (In these instances, getting out is the best immediate solution to the problem. There are a number of places where men and women can go to find help with getting out of an abusive relationship. One resource is the National Domestic Violence Hotline at: 1 (800) 799-7233 (SAFE) or www.ndvh.org).

These are all serious issues. Abuse doesn't just stop by itself. You have to make it stop. Anger doesn't just disappear. You have to work at lessening it, figure out how to diffuse it—or you have to find an appropriate way to communicate it to the person who causes those feelings. If you're able to let go of some of the baggage you've been carrying around, you'll find that it will make a huge difference in your relationships.

BLACK MEN SPEAK V:
MARRIAGE FROM A MAN'S PERSPECTIVE

My friends are my family, and one of the things that I cherish most in life is spending time with them. When I was doing research for this book, the only regret I had was that the weekends on the road were taking a toll on eye-to-eye time with my friends. Then I realized I could do both—catch up and research. I called three of my best friends and suggested we have a "guys weekend." We chose Miami since we could all get there easily. The deal I made with them was that we'd spend Saturday night at the steakhouse discussing issues of marriage and relationships, and then I would treat for a night out at the club. My buddies asked only that if they were included in the book they could remain anonymous, so I will call them Jordan, Brian, and Andre, which are their actual names. Their wives I'll keep anonymous.

Andre has been married for twelve years, Brian for five, but he is now divorced. Jordan was single during most of our friendship but fell madly in love and married three years ago. We ordered a bottle of a great cabernet from Washington State and every side dish the place had, along with a huge porterhouse, prime rib, and lamb chops. Then I asked them to open up. I started with Andre, because he had been the first among us to get married.

"We're in therapy," Andre announced to the table.

Oh, damn, I thought. *What have I opened up here?*

"It's great," he continued. "We are in a marriage group that opens up dialogue. I didn't start understanding my wife until about three years into the marriage. I realized that she was a completely different woman from the woman I thought I had married. My wife and I decided that divorce is not an option, and that was critical, 'cause most people would say, 'You aren't who I thought I married; good-bye.' We said, *no matter what*, we will *not* get divorced."

I thought the best thing at that point was to turn to Jordan quickly because, since he was most recently married, I assumed he had a lot of rough patches to adjust to after being single so long.

"I just love her like God loved the church . . . but most people take the wrong meaning from that. . . . That means you have to understand *how* God loved the church. That means I gotta forgive and not hold grudges. The key to a successful marriage is the ability to *forgive* and *not hold grudges*."

"Exactly," Andre said, "not domination, which some people

use the Bible for in their marriage, but to love and forgive and learn, and then love more. It took me years to realize that my wife had developed her perceptions about marriage from how her father was to her. He wasn't really there, so if she saw signs of that in me—any sign of her dad—alarms went off. I wasn't conscious of setting those alarms off. I realized that what my wife needed was validation and comforting. That's what *she* needed. I always perceived her as so strong and educated, which she is, but I made the mistake of thinking that equaled emotional toughness, so when she came at me with a strong posture on something, I would come back at her the same way and thought she could handle it, but she couldn't; it set off her alarms, and the emotions would escalate. She needed comforting and validation and not me just coming at her the same way she had with me. As soon as I realized that and behaved differently in those situations, she would chill out and we would make progress in whatever we were discussing instead of escalating the tension."

"I wish I'd had that kind of moment," Brian said. "I've never said this to any of you, but I felt like a failure when my marriage ended. She had the affair and it would be easy to blame her, but I had my faults. I've been able to forgive her even after the marriage was over, so, yeah, the funny thing is, once you've loved someone like that, it's still about forgiveness, and I don't think I was prepared for someone new in my life until I let go of that anger."

"So is marriage as hard work as everyone says?" I asked the table.

"Nothing that good is easy," Jordan answered. "Staying fit is hard, too. Just because something is hard doesn't mean it's not worth it; maybe the opposite is true."

"I felt like a boy before I was married," Andre confessed; "now I feel like a man. Not because of the easy stuff, but because of the hard stuff. I feel alive because I'm in this union with another person."

"But the fun of being married ran out pretty quick for me." Brian was laughing now, but I could not stop thinking that this was the first time he had sat a table and spoke out loud about his ex-wife's affair. "We got married," he continued, "and then it was like, 'What do we do next?' but there is no next; you've made that commitment, so you better know that next is the rest of your lives, so you're invested in each other's happiness. We didn't really know that, and that's the real reason we ain't together."

"So is love just one thing that goes into the choice of getting married?" I asked.

"Hill," Jordan said, "to love someone *is a choice*. Love is a feeling and a choice, together. I choose to love my wife even when I don't like her in a particular moment. I never took a relationship from a spiritual standpoint before this. I never really looked at what it meant for me to be a man with a woman. We started reading and studying the Bible together—really studying it and discussing it and praying together. That saved our marriage, meaning that we found that thing Andre just talked about, where we really understood something about each other and took it to the next level. I never let her truly know me before, 'cause if she hurt me I would man all up and not reveal. And me not showing any emotion would make her more upset. . . . So she said she would take lower and lower blows at me just to try to get me to show emotion, and that would make me man up more. For me, the man, if I didn't talk about some problem for three weeks, I was good, 'cause then I'd forget about it, but for her it festers inside. We were total opposites. I needed distance when I was upset, and she needed closeness. We tried to deal with problems, internally in two opposite ways, so both of us would just make it worse for the other. Understanding yourself is really important, even if you just begin to understand yourself, but if you don't make the effort, then you'll never understand your mate, or worse, you'll never know why, what, and how you are upsetting them. If I don't know some of me, how can she ever know any of me? I know I got emotions, but I never felt comfortable tapping into them or talking about them before now, except with you guys, you know, over wine."

That was my cue to order another bottle, because my friends and I were really talking about things now, and as I responded to the emotions at the table, I'd almost forgotten that I was writing this book for a second. After ordering, I got back to the more specific question I wanted to ask.

"What's the biggest thing we men and women don't realize about each other?" I asked.

Brian raised his hand like we were back in college. "The truth is, and I'd never admit this in mixed company, but men are more emotionally needy than females in a lot of ways. A man showing a woman his vulnerability is critical for a relationship to work, but most of us never learned that and most women don't know how to create space for a man to do it. The way women do it for each other is beautiful, but doesn't work with a man."

Andre grabbed hold of Brian's hand and clasped it; then he nodded to me and Jordan. "Exactly. Sisters have to communicate. Women have a notion that you are just supposed to understand them. They are just as guilty of not communicating as we are. I hear it when they talk to their girlfriends. They think they communicate 'cause they talk to them, but that's not the same as talking to us. That's just letting steam out to someone else. And you can't talk to us the way you talk to your girls. The crazy thing is, if they applied the same rules they do with their girls to communicating to us, then we would communicate back. What do I mean? You all know! A lot of times when they want to talk to their girls they will go to places that they enjoy, where they can relax, like the spa or shopping. If they did the same thing with us, they would create the space—the environment—for us to communicate, too. Like if they took us to a sports bar to have a beer, where we can relax. Then we could talk more easily. We would feel safe to speak about things more vulnerably."

"Right," Jordan said, "instead of always confronting us at home or when we're about to get on a plane. A woman knows how to get a man to react. I think we're pretty easy to figure out. The woman needs a little patience and can't get angry if we don't react exactly as she wants, especially if she doesn't pick her spots. My thing is public eruptions at a restaurant or confrontation the moment I walk through the door."

"The hardest thing in the world to get a brother to say," added Brian, "is 'I feel like this when you do this.' Instead of always talking in absolutes, I learned to say, 'I feel like this when you do this'; then it's not about conduct or judgment, but about feeling and perception."

> I realized that there are some married men that talk badly about marriage and their wives. From my perspective, as a single man, if that's all you hear, why would you ever want to get married? But our roundtable that night in Miami was something completely different. I was hearing a whole lot of reasons why marriage, with love, is a life-affirming experience. Here my best friends—even the divorced one—were talking

about where they were coming from without trashing marriage or their wives.

Another revelation happened well after we got the bill. No one wanted to go to the club, which, after all, was going to be my treat. Everyone wanted to stay—my friends and I—together at the table talking about what mattered most.

PART 5:
THE WAY FORWARD

FROM THE DESK OF HILL HARPER

2/21

- In the car heading to see
Nichole, I wish it could fly.

- I like what my married
friends have.

- My fear is real, but if I don't
try, I'll never know. And this could
be an amazing opportunity lost.

- She encourages me.
- We laughed and joked all night
long.
-- She is becoming my good friend.

I'm all in and it _feels good_!!

18.

The Conversation Party

Life may not be the party we hoped for, but while we're here we should dance.

—Unknown

It was the perfect night for a party, one of those indescribable nights in Southern California. I was looking forward to an eventful evening—an evening of fun with old friends and new ones, catching up and getting to know one another—but with one little catch. I wanted to inspire open communication between men and women. I didn't want to be a hypocrite and not follow through on my own advice. I wanted to create an environment where men and women could come together and speak frankly about how we can address our relationship issues—one topic at a time.

I decided to invite an interesting mix of folks. All I needed to do was provide great food, music, and cocktails, and, I hoped, my friends would provide insightful conversation. I wanted to create an atmosphere in which everyone would instantly feel comfortable and at ease. One of my favorite musicians, the incomparable Sade, helped with that. With her in mind, I created a "Soothe and Smooth" playlist on my iPod to ensure the music was right for the evening's festivities. *Music? Check.*

Since I didn't want to kill my friends with my cooking, I decided to go all out and hire a chef for the evening. Man, was that the best idea! The chef prepared an amazing menu with some of my favorites! He even included Nichole's favorite dessert—red velvet cupcakes! *Food? Check.*

The lighting was perfect and the wine was decanted—all I needed was for my guests to arrive. Since I wanted to ensure that we had an open and honest dialogue throughout the night, I had invited a diverse group of individuals. Some were single, some courting, and some married; but everyone had a strong opinion on relationships and how men and women should operate within them.

The e-invitation looked like this:

HILL'S CONVERSATION PARTY

Please join me for a night of good food, good friends, and good conversation.

———

February 15, 2009

———

8 o'clock in the evening

———

Hill's Residence

———

Los Angeles, CA

———

Please RSVP by February 10.

Include your age (your REAL age), gender, ethnicity, relationship status, and three physical attributes and three personal attributes that best describe you. Upload your pic, too!

The responses were quick and interesting. Social networking has definitely made many people less shy and more eager to publicly share. It seemed that the women would outnumber the men, but I was pretty confident that the outspoken group of brothers whom I'd been chatting with as I put together the rest of the book would be able to hold their own with the equally opinionated ladies. Don was scheduled to be in town the following week, and I convinced Robin to let him come in early to participate. Jordan was in town, and Brian and Andre flew in, so the Miami steakhouse crew was reassembled.

And of course, I invited Nichole.

After their arrival, and a quick—and delicious—dinner, we all settled in my living room with our coffee and wine and simply started talking. Although I knew it wasn't necessary, especially given the drinks and my extremely opinionated guests, I decided to create a game that would ensure a healthy and rowdy conversation. I handed out a piece of paper to everyone in the group and asked them to write down a question that they would like to ask the opposite sex regarding relationships. Once they completed this task, I simply collected all the questions and put them in a basket with questions I had already created on my own. I mixed them up, chose a question, and directed the question to my friends. Here's what happened . . .

Hill: Thank you all so much for coming out tonight. You could have chosen anywhere in the world to be, and you chose to be here. I hope you are enjoying the

wine and the company so far. And I really hope you enjoy this conversation as much as you all enjoyed those red velvet cupcakes. I can't believe all those bad boys are gone! Don't make me have to check any purses on the way out, ladies! If you think I'm playing, you see that quiet, petite woman in the corner? She's official red velvet security; all goodies must be eaten on the premises or you will get body searched. Just kidding. That's actually Dr. Tanya, a relationship and couples therapist, who will be observing the goings-on. But, since I am always the curious one, before we officially begin, I'm interested to know your expectations for the evening. Why did each of you decide to come to this party tonight?

Eric: The free food! And all the actresses you know are hot, so . . . the chicks of course . . .

Brad: What my good buddy here meant to say is that we came here tonight to enjoy some enlightening conversation with some beautiful and intelligent women.

Trace: There you go. Your friend said what he meant the first time, and you know it! Then you had to start spouting off some straight-up bullshit. So-called men refusing to speak the truth when they are asked a clear and direct damn question. What is so hard about that!? Ugh, it's so frustrating.

Brad: Good Lord. I was not trying to offend you, but you want some honesty? Okay, well, you must be one of those women with a serious chip on your shoulder.

Sarita: Oh, not at all. It's cool. Your friend is handsome. And funny. Some people can't take a joke.

Hill: All right, while these four play musical chairs, does anybody else care to share what prompted them to come tonight?

Brian: I thought we were going to the club.

Andre: This is cheaper than therapy.

Hill: Very funny. Anyone else? What prompted you to come tonight, Nichole?

Nichole: You invited me! You know I'm always down to support you. Plus, the idea sounded really interesting. To me at least . . .

Erica: Better than spending yet another Friday night alone.

Brad: I've noticed many of the best women either stay at home or just go out to eat or the movies with their girlfriends. How am I supposed to meet them?

Jason: I am in church every Sunday, wanna meet a nice girl, and I still have not found the one I'm looking for.

Aishah: Well, you might need to change your church, sweetie, because I'm in worship every Sunday, and I'm a good woman.

Tami: He must go to the early service. I work hard all week, so I deserve to go out and play at night. Going to the clubs does not mean I don't love the Lord. I just know how to enjoy the life God has blessed me to live on Saturday, and also how to thank him for letting me live it on Sunday.

Hill: Don, I know you have a pretty strong perspective on Black male and female relationships. As the person here who has been married by far the longest, care to kick things off before we dive into the questions?

Don: Look at the way people are interacting here; you can see it. I think these problems come out of our history. Lemme explain it this way. Take a White couple and Black couple, say, "White Fred and Wilma versus Black Fred and Wilma." Here's the scenario. Fred goes out drinking with his friends one night. He tells Wilma he'll be home by midnight. Midnight comes and goes; Fred's not back. Guess what? He hasn't called either. Two in the morning, Fred waltzes in, drunk and happy. He gives Wilma a sloppy kiss. "Sorry I'm late, babe. I was hanging with the guys and lost track of time."

Simple situation we can probably all relate to. Any woman would be upset, and most guys would try to act like it's no big deal. There definitely needs to be a discussion, but the difference in how it might go down can easily illustrate the unique dynamic at work in Black relationships.

White Wilma sits up in bed, clearly not having gone to sleep, and obviously pissed. She reads Fred the riot act. "You're such an asshole. You couldn't call? You couldn't take sixty seconds away from your partying to call me, and let me know you're still alive? Show some common decency, Fred!"

It starts the same way with Black Wilma, except she doesn't just direct her anger at Black Fred; she's got something to say about Black men in general.

"You're just a wannabe player. You were probably out there trying to hook up with a White girl! *Typical Black man*. No respect for Black women!"

Somehow what should have been a discussion between and about individuals becomes an indictment of Black men as a group. White Fred only has to defend himself. It might not be easy, but it pales in comparison to Black Fred's task. Black Fred must speak for the entire pantheon of Black men, past and present. Or, if Black Fred's not careful, he can fall into the trap of sacrificing his own heritage in order to save himself, by insisting he's not a "typical Black man." Sounds good at first, until you realize that's the equivalent of saying good Black men are the exception.

I know y'all have been around for the aftermath of these kinds of discussions and you know Black men make the same mistake. When White Fred complains to his friends about how Wilma was riding his ass for staying out late, he'll say, "Sometimes I can't stand Wilma; she nags too much." Again, he's not making a blanket statement about White women. He's talking about his girl and her issues. But when Black Fred gets around his friends, you hear him say, "I can't stand sisters; they nag too much." Black Wilma takes the hit for all Black women. Black Fred and Wilma's overreactions have turned a common and minor relationship problem into a major issue about the compatibility of Black men and women.

Hill: Okay . . . Let's dip into the bowl and get the conversation party started! The first official question is . . .

What do you think is the main thing women don't realize about men?

Anybody want to jump in . . . ?

Kyle: Women don't have a clue. What women don't realize is that all y'all do is talk amongst yourselves, giving each other misinformation. For instance, a woman tells other women that if they cook good, look good, and sex their men good, they'll keep their men happy. And, yes, all that stuff is good, but I and almost every guy wants a woman who is a cheerleader for him—encourages him, makes him feel like he can conquer the world—over all that other stuff. And women don't get that. They don't.

Hill: All right, all right. Let's keep it flowing. Next question.

Describe sexy. And, what makes you feel sexy?

Aishah: I know the questions are anonymous, but I don't mind saying it's my question, and I'm never scared to start. Simply stated, sexy is . . . me. And men who know how to work what they got is what makes me feel sexy.

Hill: Haha. Okay. I'm not mad atcha! How about some more detail?

Aishah: It's like this: When I look in the mirror, and I see what God has gifted me with—the front, the back—and I see the men's stares, I can't help but feel sexy.

I know that these curves can break the strongest man down into tears.

Trace: See, that's not sexy at all to me. Sexy is in a man's swagger. Seeing him and thinking that he might be able to completely dominate you. Most women are naturally sexy by nature. Men have to try; we don't. We know we hold that power of the P that makes the world go round. That's why we walk the way we do. Walking down the street turning heads makes me feel sexy. Sometimes watching the right women with that right power turns my head.

Lloyd: My fiancée, Dana, made me work to get her attention. That was sexy to me. I felt like she must be something special, and thinking about finding out more about her, what lay beyond her beautiful figure and appearance, was sexy—is sexy—to me. Less is sometimes more sexy.

Zee: Hey, wait . . . Trace, did you say *women* walking down the street make you feel sexy?

Trace: I'm bi.

Zee: Oh. Hill, that's sexy! A bi chick? Oh, yes, two is always better than one. This woman's sexy appeal just went up in stock points. A lot of women don't have open minds—especially Black women—so it's sexy when you come across one who does.

Hill: Iyana, did you have something you wanted to add? I'm watching your face, and it has changed expressions a few times.

Iyana: Well, honestly, since you asked, this whole conversation just confuses me. She doesn't want him and she's sexier now? She likes women maybe more than men, and she's sexier now? That just does not make sense to me.

Kyle: Okay, well, let me see if I can help you out and break a man's mind down in thirty seconds or less. Sex equals sexy. Double the women, you double the sex, you double the sexy. I know, we men can be such pigs, but that's the honest truth. I agree with Trace. Most women have an innate sex appeal. Sexy to me is a woman's hair, how she smells, how she touches you, even in casual conversation. Maybe when she is laughing, she reaches over and touches your arm, or when you kiss her, she will reach up and caress your face just right. Women are so soft and elegant without trying. When they wear soft fabrics like silk or cashmere, yes, indeed, that is sexy right there. We men can be a bunch of rough, raw, and scruffy mugs. So sexy is anything that is the opposite of us. I feel sexy when I catch women staring at me. Even when they try to slide their eyes away, I feel sexy knowing that something I got made them look. Kinda puffs a brotha up inside.

Jason: Iyana, if I could also address what you said . . . I would have to agree with mostly everything you mentioned. I'm a monogamous type of man, which is why I also have to agree with my brother Zee when he said meeting an open-minded woman is sexy. I'm looking for a wife, and a lifetime is a long, long time to spend with just one person. There is nothing foul, sinful, or shameful about the marriage bed, so knowing a woman has an open outlook on things of the sensual nature is definitely sexy. Because you have got to keep it fresh.

Dana: Sexy to me is my husband. It seemed like he could just take me. And I feel sexy when I'm being taken. Also when I am all done up at my best. Nice hair, nice outfit. I guess in that way, I'm kind of a girl's girl.

Nichole: Yes, love. There is nothing like a new bag to make a girl feel sexy. Seriously, stores can be sexy for a woman. The right shoes, with the right jewelry, with the right bag, can make a woman dang near come with its sex appeal.

Zee: Wait a minute . . . are you saying inanimate objects are sexy?

Nichole: Sometimes. Many times. Well, yes. Sometimes inanimate objects are sexier, and less messy than a man.

Trace: I agree.

Nichole: If you want to get deeper, sexy is when you feel good. Sexy to me is when a man feels good about himself, because it is projected into everything that he does. He is wrapped up in his sexy, and most of the time men do not even know it. I feel sexy when I feel I am at my best. So that's what sexy is to me.

Hill: Okay, okay. Eric, Sarita, you two can be the last ones to respond to this question before we move on. I see you enjoying those cheesecake bites together, though, so I don't want to interrupt.

Eric: Oh, no, it's all good. Sexy to me is a woman who can be herself. Sexy is nice, and welcoming, and knowing how to have fun. Sexiness is more than physical. And if she knows how to lick cheesecake off her fingers just right? That's a hard-to-find sexy right there.

Sarita   (licking her fingers): Wooow. Let me get this napkin. Listen, I am not a fashionista, but I do feel sexy when I dress up in my Sunday morning or Saturday night best. High heels, favorite perfume; those things make me feel good about myself.

Eric: Yes! Hallelujah for high heels.

Sarita   (laughing): Yes, stilettos are sexy. As for a man? Just a well-groomed, nice, confident man is sexy to me.

Hill: Okay, that did pop things off indeed. Thank you, Aishah.

Aishah: It's what I do. And y'all can stop being so formal. Just call me Big Sexy.

Hill: Okay, Big Sexy, let's see where this next question will take us.

Sarita: Wait! Can we talk about monogamy? We know that half the guys in this room are into threesomes and stuff, but I just want to settle down with a monogamous, faithful man. Let's talk about *that* for a minute.

Jordan: Are monogamous and faithful two different things?

Sarita: No.

Jordan: Oh.

Hill: Okay. Can men be faithful and monogamous?

Eric: I've been faithful in all of my relationships. If you decide to be faithful, you'll be faithful.

Don: People who are fulfilled have no reason to stray.

Kyle: I think it's sometimes hard for men to commit for a lot of different reasons. It might be because of the men or women in their life, past history . . . we are all creatures of environment, so all I can say is look to whom a man or woman interacts with or surrounds themselves with.

Chris: I am faithful and monogamous because I love being married. It is the *best*, yet most difficult, thing in existence. I believe this even more than raising children, as they will ultimately move on with their own lives at some point. In-laws and other connections will ultimately pass on, leaving the union between you two, which by our nature is something that always needs to be cultivated. But I would not trade it for the world; nothing worth having is not worth fighting for.

Hill: Okay, good. Next question.

Do you think that the man should always be the main breadwinner in a relationship?

Aishah: I work hard, hard, hard. But yet, I still have barely enough to pay my bills. Having two incomes would greatly increase my quality of life. So like you guys were saying earlier about two ladies being together is sexy? Well, I think two incomes together are sexy.

Brad: See, that answer sends up a major red flag for me.

Aishah: Why would me wanting two incomes send you a red flag? I'm willing to contribute mine to the pot. I'm not just there to lie on my back, then get up expecting cash for services rendered. I would think that would be a great thing!

Brad: That's not the part that was the red flag. Why do you work so hard but still not have enough to pay your bills? It makes me wonder. You're so focused on trying to be sexy, buying sexy clothes, buying sexy furniture, buying sexy cars. . . . Shoot, do you even own a sexy home while you are out spending all that dirty, sexy money? How is your credit being impacted by this sexy lifestyle you have chosen to lead? You're thinking a second income will give you more. But in the end, will your habits make your partner have less?

Aishah: Dang, brother, you thought about all of that, that quickly?

Brad: I most certainly did. How a woman handles her finances is important.

Tami: My mother always taught me, no romance without finance. I'm independent, and I don't really need a man. But trust and believe, if I do spend my quality time with one, he is going to have to come out of the pockets in appreciation of my attention.

Brandi: Exactly! I can be broke all by myself. My man has to be the main breadwinner. What's yours is mine, and what's mine is mine. I got bills to pay!

Zee: That's probably part of the reason you are by yourself now. Most men got their eyes out for women like you.

Iyana: The reality is that finances are a major aspect of a relationship. A solid marriage is not based and built on love alone. Unfortunately, that is one of the things I have learned the hard way. Finances are actually one of the main reasons that my ex is my ex—it became a major issue. I work hard, I save, and I invest. He was the polar opposite. While we were dating, I thought his habits were cute, daring, and a sign that he could perhaps loosen me up a little. But after we married, both of our FICO scores tanked. Brandi, when you get married, there is no such thing as "what's yours is mine, and what's mine is mine." Everything's connected. And when his spending habits caused his financial destruction, mine was right there next to him at the bottom of the credit-score pile. Our divorce was over three years ago, and I am still paying the price.

Eric: That's scary. I was not really taught about finances and how to build good credit. I don't think most of us men have been. Through trial and error, I have managed to create a nice nest egg for myself. I would hate to find a nice woman with bad financial sense and have it all crumble down.

Chris: Listen. I've been married for ten years. I will say that having an excellent understanding of your partner's spending habits and creating a monthly and long-term financial plan can make all the difference in the world. Like Iyana, my wife and I have seen many of our friends' marriages end because of arguments over money. That is one of the areas that a couple *must* be on the same page with from the beginning, or, in my opinion, their relationship will not succeed.

Zee: See, that's all I'm saying! I'm just not trying to get involved with a woman that will bring me down!

Nichole: Zee, maybe you are approaching it the wrong way. Just something to consider . . . instead of approaching it from the negative—"Oh, she gonna bring me down"—maybe you could shift your thinking toward "Let me find a woman that can help bring me up." You'll be looking for the same financial qualities, but I think the mental spin you put on it can make a huge difference in the outcome.

Lloyd: I've been on the wrong side of the law, trying to amass that quick buck so I could impress those women looking for the dude with the car, the fly gear, poppin' the bottles at the club. I paid a heavy price for that mentality. I thought if I was broke, no woman would want me. And can you believe that in my mind, broke was driving an Acura instead of a big-body Benz. I just had my values all screwed up. But God is good, man. This woman right here met me at my lowest, when I didn't have anything. I was actually going in when we reconnected. We knew each other as kids, and she still saw the best in me through that situation. I got out with no job and nowhere to go. And she was right there. She took me in. To her mama's house. She had just graduated from USC, had her first teaching gig. I couldn't believe that she was giving me even half a second of her time. She encouraged me to rise above my past. Finding a job was hard, but coming home with nothing to contribute was harder. She made it clear that if I chose to go back to my old ways, we would be over. The love of a good woman can change your life. I got a little nine-to-five gig. Small change compared to what I had been pulling before, but in the end that small change made big things. We poured ours in together, got a joint savings account. And we saved, for about two years. Both of our paychecks were going to paying down her bills and saving. Seven years later, we are buying our second property. I own an Escalade, my lady has a nice little convertible, and it's all legal.

Hill: That's an amazing story, man . . .

Lloyd: It's real. I see the jealous glint in some of her so-called friends' or coworkers' eyes. All they see is the end result, though. They wouldn't have given me a second look if they met me when she did. I have to hold her down. She has a lifetime of getting spoiled by me—and I don't mean with stuff. I spoil her with all I have to give. A real man will take care of his woman better than he takes care of himself.

Jason: You are a blessed man, brother.

Hill: Dana, what was it like from your perspective? Why and how were you able to look past everything so many women are conditioned to look for in a man?

Dana: If I had not known him before, I can assure you, I wouldn't have given him the time of day. I mean, he was goin' into jail two months before I graduated with honors from one of California's top schools. Did I spend all that time to wait outside a jail to scoop up some random brother? No. But, like I said, I knew Lloyd. We grew up together. I knew he got caught up in a bad situation. But what was endearing was that he was not making excuses. He always owned up to his bad choices and had a plan for when he got out. When he got out, he never made an empty promise. There was never a moment of "I can't get a job because I got a record," or whatever. He just quietly took it like a man and went out every day until he got something. He is truly all a man should be in every sense of the word. He protects, he provides, and I consider myself blessed to have him in my life. We are in this thing together for the long haul, through good times and bad. Yeah, a lot of people see our end result. They are not seeing the struggle and trust it took to get here. Trust me, people thought I was crazy for choosing to be with this man. They thought he would use me, leave me, or always be nothing but a dead weight. But I had faith that he was more than his circumstances. Even more, just like I helped him, he helped me. Women should give men a chance if their actions match up with their words.

Brandi: Awww . . . that's beautiful! Y'all are like a real-life fairy tale! I want that!

Dana: It's about more than wanting it. You have to be willing to work for it. We went to premarital counseling and financial counseling. We planned our work, then worked our plan. I guess that, sometimes, you have to be willing to wait for it. I mean, you have to be willing to wait for the right man and for what you are trying to achieve in the greater span of your life, over the long term, not just in the here and the now.

Nichole: Amen to that. There is absolutely nothing wrong with waiting for that one you are equally yoked with. Dana, it is wonderful to hear how your story has worked out. It really is, but for me, I have a great credit score, I have a great career, and I am waiting until the man who I feel is a good match for me comes into my life. To me, this means that he will value similar qualities. But that's just me.

Brad: I feel the same way. I do not mind helping a woman up, but when we meet, I will get all of her financial facts up front so that I can be sure that her financial situation will not bring me down. I know it sounds wrong or politically incorrect for me to say that. Yeah, we can build together. But I am not going to get involved with a woman that because of her financial choices is going to start us off with a handicap. And a prenup is a must.

Brandi: Oh, here we go. Prenup? That is so not romantic. So what you are saying is that you are committing to marriage while expecting to get divorced? Great!

Brad: No, what I am saying is this: I am marrying you with a sense of reality. I've been down the aisle and back, and I am so thankful that I did have a prenuptial agreement. I can only imagine how much more difficult that period of my life would have been if we had not had one.

Lloyd: Well, for Dana and me, divorce is not an option, so there was no need for a prenup.

Dana: When you intend to share the rest of your life with someone, you should be committed completely. Not having a prenup enforces that perspective.

Zee: Well, that's all nice for y'all. My dude found his Cinderella. Meanwhile the rest of us are left out here with more chicken heads than princesses.

Trace: And we women are left out here with more no-good muthaf . . . you know what? I'm not even going to take it there. Lloyd and Dana, I think it's great that y'all have what you do. It gives a little hope to the rest of us out here struggling.

Tami: Whaaat? Did I just hear Miss All-Men-Are-No-Good just say she has a little hope?

Trace: Of course. I need hope. I am at my wits' end. I have lived my life thinking the right man—my Dr. Huxtable, Mr. Big, Prince Charming—was right around the corner. I've rode a lotta dicks and kissed a lotta pricks looking for my Mr. Right. And they all been Mr. Wrong, Mr. Wronger, and Mr. Wrongest.

Sarita: I hear what you are saying. I mean, just like men we can get caught up. My finances are not the best. I was a young single mother. My whole adult life has been about robbing Peter to pay Paul. So does that mean I don't deserve the love of a good man? Does that mean that Nichole is better than me because her credit score is?

Brad: Yes.

Zee: Yes.

Eric: Not necessarily.

Hill: Eric?

Eric: I mean, it is ideal that you meet someone right on the same page as you, but what are the odds of that? Like that couple right there, Dana and Lloyd. Now, we're all holding them up as the barometer of successful Black love and the all-American dream. But did y'all hear the brother? He went to prison when they first met. Then they stayed with her mama for a few years! And her credit was jacked! I just think we got to get out of this microwave mind-set expecting something to be ready-made when *we* are ready for it to be. Sarita, if a woman is hardworking, willing to pull her weight, and recognize her role in her mistakes, I am open to helping to support and do what we can to build a financial and hopefully loving future together. I mean, ah . . . when that time comes, of course. Till then, a brotha is looking for the biggest butt and a smile!

Hill (laughing): Okay, so let's move on to the next question . . .

For a divorced man—What ended your marriage?

Hill: Brian, you've been awfully quiet. You care to take this one on?

Brian: Sure. I've had enough liquor so I will just tell the truth. What ended my marriage? This might make you laugh, but what ended my marriage was me walking around my house naked. Sometimes I used to like to just walk around my crib with no clothes on and just let my stomach and everything hang out, ya know? Relaxed, chill. Lay back on the couch and watch TV. There's no better feeling than letting your stomach and your dick hang out. After we got married, the first time my wife saw me do this, she sucked her teeth and let out a snicker and said, "Put some clothes on." She will never know how bad she hurt my feelings. And my never-let-'em-see-you-sweat male ego said I could never tell her. I stopped walking around the house naked and never did it again. You know what's weird? I never felt truly comfortable again. And I didn't stop doing it because I let her tell me what I could and couldn't do; I stopped because she ridiculed me for something I really enjoyed. Something that relaxed me, and I probably enjoyed it more than anything else I ever did. I think women try to act like they have a monopoly on being the ones that get hurt, but they hurt men bad, too. Just in different ways. And we never let them know, we just check out and that's what I did.

What is the difference between having sex and making love?

Andre: Wait, Hill, can we ask you something?

Hill: No.

I saw the Miami steakhouse crew look at Nichole and me and, more important, look at me looking at Nichole. I recalled that I may have mentioned something about her in Miami.

Jordan: Have you fallen in love in the past few months?

Hill: Yes.

There it was. I answered that question pretty quickly because I was caught off guard and didn't have time to think of a clever reply. But knowing my boys, I should have known that they weren't going to let me off that easy. They hit me with a question that I never would have expected from them.

Andre: Over this past number of months, studying relationships, what's the biggest thing you've learned about *yourself*?

I'm not sure if it was the wine or the fact that I was inspired by everyone else's honesty or the simple fact that I really had come to believe in the intrinsic value of being embarrassingly honest, but I answered his question with no cover.

Hill: I used to say that I needed to be *in* love with a woman to commit to her. Only if I felt "in love" would I believe that she "deserved" my love. But with that childish thinking I never realized that love is a *choice*. We are not "in" or "out" of love; we choose to be either "in" or "out." We choose to commit or not. Realizing this, I was confronted with the question— How could I ever choose to love someone else unless I truly love myself? I used to front and present all this bravado and ego, as if I loved me, but I didn't. So I collected women to try and build up my false ego and fill the emptiness of not allowing myself to go "all in" with someone. I'm choosing to commit. I'm choosing to love. I'm choosing to be vulnerable. I have to *do*, before I can *be*.

After I finished, everyone was quiet for what, to me, seemed like an eternity, but was probably two seconds. And just that quickly, Nichole squeezed my hand and someone else was already being asked the next question out of the hat.

My iPod continued to loop my Sade playlist; I heard "No Ordinary Love" start up again for the third time. And my game continued late into the night. . . .

THE MORNING-AFTER DEBRIEFING

The next morning, my head was still spinning, and not just from all the wine I'd drunk the night before. I think I had a conversation hangover.

To make sense of it all, I called Dr. Tanya to talk about everything she had witnessed from the group the previous night. I sipped on my morning protein shake and shook my head. Everyone had seemed to have completely different perspectives. Not too many people agreed about anything.

"Hill, your party and the conversations that ensued were an amazing success," Dr. Tanya reassured me. "I applaud you for opening up a forum and putting those questions out there to have conversations about," she continued. "We are all different and have individual perspectives about relationships and sex. But if you're true to yourself and know that you are forever changing and growing, you will be practicing truth. And a rewarding benefit to being open and honest is attracting people who share your values, the kind of people you actually want to be around."

She was right. I was still trying to register some of the new things that I had learned, particularly about Nichole. For instance, I had no idea that she held the exact same views as I did when it came to finding a financially fit partner to build a relationship with. It was refreshing, reassuring. However, she also mentioned the fact that she didn't think she wanted to get married. Not only was I surprised; I couldn't believe that she hadn't shared that with me before. Couldn't she trust me? Dr. Tanya said, "Did you ever *ask* her about her views on marriage?" Of course I hadn't. I had only made assumptions. "No," I said.

Then it dawned on me. Here I was, expecting Nichole to have shared this with me, assuming that she hadn't yet broached the subject because she didn't *want* to. Instead, I began to realize how I was also contributing to the lack of communication. If I wondered about something—whether it was something as silly as finding out her favorite ice cream flavor or something as serious as knowing whether she planned to marry, or would consider relocating to L.A. to further develop our relationship—all I had to do was ask.

There was another beneficial outcome from the conversation party. A few people exchanged numbers, and I think that Eric and Sarita already have a date lined up!

But I think the most important moment came to me late at night after everyone had left. Just a few months earlier I had been at the Blakes'. From that moment on, as you know from reading, two things had stuck in my mind. One was Nichole. The other was the life, spirit, and environment the Blakes had built that I thought was something that had slipped away from our culture and my generation.

The conversation party had produced the same feeling I'd had at the Blake's, the feeling of belonging, of communal intimacy. It was possible all along among my friends, but we hadn't made the move to make it happen, I guess because for whatever reason it didn't come easily to us. But that night was the closest experience of it's kind I'd had since the night in D.C.

The other thing I remember about the Blakes' was the sadness and intense lonely solitude I'd felt when I'd gotten into my rental car and looked at my image in the rearview mirror. The night of the conversation party, Nichole and I fell asleep holding each other's hand.

It was the least lonely I've felt in a very long time.

19.

Man Up!

———— ⚜ ————

We need to internalize this idea of excellence. Not many folks spend a lot of time trying to be excellent.

—President Barack Obama,
married to First Lady Michelle Obama since 1992

So here's a reality: Just because our better judgment tells us to do something, it doesn't mean that we always do it. Just because our doctors tell us to take certain measures or to stop certain habits in order to improve our health, it doesn't mean we always listen or follow the plan word for word. We might still sneak in a pork chop or two, a plate of mac and cheese, or a huge slice of red velvet cake. Every pack of cigarettes comes with the surgeon general's warning on the box, but we are still buying them.

People don't always do what's in their own best interest, so it would stand to reason that they definitely aren't always doing what's in the best interest of the people in their lives. What men say we want does not always sync up with the actions we take, especially when presented with certain types of temptation. I try to remember my grandfather's advice "If you don't wanna get stung, don't hang with bees." I know as a man there are times when I am weak, so, as I've matured, I try not to put myself around hornet nests or beehives. It seems that's what growing into manhood is—making choices about in what ways we want to live our lives.

I want to talk very seriously about one specific area where we as Black men have truly failed one another and failed Black women. We have failed in the area of Black male responsibility and accountability. I realize that this proclamation may lead to a whole lot of my brothers out there being upset with me—but the truth is the truth. We as Black men rarely hold other men accountable when we clearly see that they are not living up to their responsibilities with the women they are dating or married to and, even worse, with the children they have fathered. It's easier to look the other way, pretend to not notice what's going on, or to make excuses for a friend. At times, we even cover for them.

I'm ashamed to admit it, but I've done it before myself; I've watched a friend of mine snuggle up to his girlfriend, the woman he claims is the love of his life, and I've watched her receive that affection not having the slightest idea that another woman had been holding him and kissing him in that same way less than twenty-four hours before.

Every time that we as Black men are silent in the face of mistreatment of women by other men, even men who are our friends, every time we are complicit in helping our male friends cause their women pain and, less apparently, when we are complicit in that brother's self-sabotage, we are not just consenting to that behavior; we are condoning it. We're saying, "It's okay to treat a woman like that." But what if that woman was your sister, your cousin, your best friend? Would silence seem appropriate then?

When my friend Julia found herself in a situation with a married man, she told me that one of the reasons she believed his lies was that his boys always backed him up. When she met the man's friends, it legitimized him and their relationship. It told her that she wasn't some little secret of his. After all, he'd introduced her to his college buddies, his friends of twenty or more years. No married man, she'd convinced herself, would do something like that. It'd be too risky. Little did she know the sort of bond that some men share.

The same guys who would have dinner with Julia and her man would probably show up the next morning at the man and his wife's house with their own wives in tow, and never once let on that he was cheating. A true friend would have reminded him that not only was he disrespecting women; he was also disrespecting himself. Men in those types of situations are not being men of their word, trustworthy, or courageous. It takes *courage* to tell a friend that he's not acting in his own self-interest, that he's about to shatter the opportunity to have a happy life with the woman he loves. It takes *courage* for a man to tell one of his boys that he's acting like a coward and that he needs to "man up!" It took me watching a woman who is my dear friend being dogged again and again by my boy to realize this. Some brothers feel talking to another man about how he treats his woman or his children would be overstepping a boundary or breaking some sort of male code. But desperate times require desperate measures. As we witness the residual damage on the family structures in our communities, in part, because of a lack of male responsibility, its time for us to hold each other accountable.

How powerful would it be for you to say, "You know, man, I don't feel comfortable with you bringing other women around when I know your lady. She and I go almost as far back as you and I do." We as men need to have the *courage* to check the behavior of our friends, or we will never see a change in the

> ✧
> Choose to be accountable.
> Choose to be responsible.
> ✧

way Black men and women relate. Can the codes and cycles that are destructive to our own growth and the growth of our relationships be broken? Yes, I think they can, but it's going to take men holding other men accountable for it to truly take hold.

These behaviors damage the relationships between men and women. For women, it can lead to them questioning themselves and not trusting other good men. It can ruin their self-esteem and the way they view themselves. We should remind women who find themselves on the wrong side of a cheating mate that it says more about his insecurities as a man than about her deficiencies. We have to step up and be honest about who some of our brothas are, or get a hold of that mirror and check ourselves.

Statistically, Black children are being raised in single-parent households in numbers that are almost double those of any other race. It is not uncommon to see men who have multiple children with multiple partners, and each child is dependent solely upon his or her mother for emotional, intellectual, spiritual, and financial support. Black men, many who were not raised by their fathers, often continue the cycle of dropping their seed without taking responsibility to nurture it so that it grows properly.

One of the complaints I've heard over and over again from the young brothers I've talked to at readings, signings, and speaking engagements is that sisters get pregnant on purpose to trap them into marriage. If a Black man is uninterested in having a child, then he has to be willing to take equal responsibility for birth control. If a man has any doubts at all about the sincerity or trustworthiness of a woman he's dating, he shouldn't be with her. At the very least he should be responsible for birth control. I've heard from a lot of women that men complain about wearing condoms and some even refuse to put them on. Many of these are the same men who don't want anything to do with the children they "accidentally" fathered.

A lot of us have made choices that we now realize were mistakes, choices that if we had to do over again we'd do differently. Some choices might cause us minor discomfort and embarrassment but do very little lasting damage. Some choices, thankfully, are completely reversible. Having a baby is not one of those. The fact that you made a mistake does not entitle you to make the larger mistake of not taking your share of the responsibility for the life you've helped to create. Children wind up being the victims.

It is an issue of responsibility, pure and simple. Brothers have told me, "Hill, I just don't have enough money to take care of a baby." But the real question is, Are they even trying? I have seen situations where the same men who cannot be bothered to put food in their children's mouths are quick to purchase the latest fashion or tech accessory for themselves. Unfortunately, a father's attachment to his child is influenced by his own experience in childhood. Maybe it happens because these men don't take the opportunity to bond in the beginning, so that the separation lasts to the point that the child

> ❦
> Children wind up
> being the victims.
> ❦

becomes a stranger. If a Black man is raised by his father, there is a greater chance he will feel accountable to his own child.

Another reason a lot of men don't like to pay child support is that they resent having to give money to a woman whom they are no longer with and from whom they are no longer getting anything. Whenever I hear brothers talking that way, I attempt to get them to shift their perspective, to look at it from another point of view. I remind them that the money they are giving to their exes is for the upkeep of their child or children, not for their ex. If they still insist that their ex uses the money for things other than the welfare of their child, I en*courage* them to be more—not less—proactive about meeting the needs of their child. I urge them to look into what safeguards can be put in place to ensure that the money they are paying really does cover those needs, and to move forward from there, rather than to simply abandon their responsibility. For instance, I tell young fathers, purchase clothes for your child yourself or give gift certificates to certain children stores if your mistrust of your ex is your real concern.

As helpful as money is when trying to raise a child, it is not the be-all and end-all. I've had friends who've boasted about how nobody could ever accuse them of being late with their child support, or how it didn't matter how many children they had as long as they provided for them all. "When's the last time you called your daughter?" I ask them. "Do you know what your son's favorite food is?"

Many men I know don't realize that all the money in the world can't replace time spent with a parent. There are famous people in the media who give child support but don't spend time with their children. At the end of the day, wouldn't that child rather have a relationship with her father, and not just his money?

What does that tell the child about her value? I'm sure that any adult Black who was raised without his or her father's physical presence would have exchanged whatever fancy gifts the father might have provided for a chance to spend a Sunday afternoon or two together. I was raised by a single parent, my father, and I know how important his presence in my life was. And even though he passed away in 2000, the residual effects of the presence of a strong male figure in my life impacts all aspects of my choices every day.

What will the woman we so want and dream of, the one who will marry us and start a family with us, think of us when she discovers that we're not taking care of the family we already have? People tend to be creatures of habit, and until we make a conscious choice not to, we tend to repeat the same patterns over and over again. A lot of women know that the best way to gauge how a man will treat them is to take note of how he treats his exes. If we men want to attract a woman who is sincere and worthy of our love, time, and attention, then we also have to be sincere and worthy of that love, time, and attention. I have friends who tell me that they won't date a man who disses his ex, because if things don't work out, they know they'll be the next ex he's talking bad about.

Last but not least, there are some men who are perpetual adolescents. They will never feel that they are ready for a monogamous relationship. To those types of men, the level of discipline monogamy requires is a level they are unwilling and unable to reach. They are like that five-year-old boy who wants the toy in the store and selfishly cannot understand why he cannot have it. I know about guys like that because I was one of them.

> ✦
> Life isn't a movie
> or a fairy tale.
> ✦

There is no doubt that relationships aren't easy; they always require sacrifices. Just because you find someone you think you want to be with doesn't mean that you're going to walk off into a beautiful sunset and be happy together forever, the end. That's why I can't stand Hollywood romantic comedies (even some of the ones I've been in). They set up unreal expectations. Life isn't a movie or a fairy tale. People run around and talk about finding "the one," as if there will be no problems once you find that "perfect" person.

Perfection doesn't exist, but what I've heard from my buddies who are blessed enough to be in solid, happy marriages is that getting through the difficult stretches makes the good parts that much sweeter. They are very clear that the hard work that is required is worth it.

I'm so ready to meet the woman who is capable of being my partner for life, the woman who believes that I am capable of being her partner for life. In the past, I have mistaken chemistry for love; I've mistaken lust for love. I have shut down and refused to fully receive or return the love that's been given to me simply because I was afraid. I've held back when I should have given more. I know this, and I've come to terms with my fear as much as I am able. I realize now that part of what we need to do to man up is to have the courage to admit that we are scared and that we are willing to change. And as men, the more of us that step up and do that the more we can support each other in the new choices that a new lifestyle will bring. Finding a life partner and acting accordingly is good.

I know I can't continue to allow my self-imposed fears to keep me single. It's time for me to grow up and to become the family man my grandparents raised and inspired me to become. I, and a lot of brothas, need to stop dating like I'm in college and get to the next level of my relationships. I don't know about you, but I am not willing to be the old man at the club—you know the one—whose age is out of step with his environment because emotionally his growth is stunted by his fear. This is an area where I know I need to man up, and I know that I am not alone. But I know growing up and being a gentle*man* is worth it.

My friend Stacey looked at me recently and longingly said, "Hill, I haven't dated a true gentleman in so long." I love the word *gentleman*. The word itself combines two very powerful sentiments. In one sense, a "gentleman" has a quality of being "gentle"—caring, loving, aware. But being a gentleman also calls on us to be a "man"—strong, decisive, energized. It is like what is described in a favorite book, by Dan Millman, *The Way of the Peaceful Warrior*. After I'd read Millman's book, one of my goals in life became to live my life as a "peaceful warrior": someone who lives life with a warrior's spirit and energy but from a peaceful place of love and supporting others. To me, living as a peaceful warrior encompasses the same ideas as living as a gentleman. Being gentle does not take away from being a man.

Too many of us put on a facade of being a man, but rarely do we express the *courage* (heart) to be gentlemen. We compete with one another over who has the most carats in their ears or biggest rims ("Dubs and up! Yeah!"), as if the kind of car we drive or how "hot" the girl we date is or how many diamonds we have somehow defines manhood. But these are all just elaborate "whose dick is bigger?" contests disguised as a "I just like nice things, man" sentiment. There is nothing wrong with liking and having nice things. I love beautiful cars—and I own a few—but there is a difference between owning something because you truly like it and owning something because you want others to see it and be impressed by it.

A gentleman is the personification of a strong man, and humility is one of the strongest attributes of a true gentleman. A great example is a man I have known for twenty years, President Obama. Ever since I have known him, he has been the personification of a gentleman, a humble person attempting to uplift others, but approaching life with a fierce warrior spirit of "we will win!" He is a gentleman, and I believe we need to man up and follow his example. So if you see a brother not acting like a gentleman, have the *courage* to explain to him how a gentleman acts. It is likely not his fault that he doesn't know; just like many of us, his father may not have been there to teach him. But the cycle must stop with us, and it can only stop if we begin insisting to one another that we man up, gentlemen!

20.

Three to Be Free

Miracles begin with relationship.

—Bishop T. D. Jakes,
married to Serita Ann Jamison since 1981

Which came first, the chicken or the egg? When I was young, I used to make myself sick trying to figure out the right answer. I'd consider both possibilities, only to find myself back at square one, realizing that it was impossible for there to be a chicken without an egg and an egg without a chicken.

I thought about that little conundrum this morning, because in some ways, I've been scratching my head with a similar kind of question. I've been wondering whether an epiphany comes before an event, or whether it's an event that actually brings on an epiphany. Obviously, it wasn't just any event and any epiphany that I had in mind. I was thinking of my epiphany earlier this year when I met Nichole, who, I'm pretty sure you've already figured out, has become extremely important to me over the last several months.

At the beginning of this journey, I thought it was the epiphany I had while driving to my hotel from the Blakes' anniversary party that made me ready for the possibility of something more than a casual friendship with Nichole. Now, having gone through this journey, I'm wondering whether meeting Nichole was what brought on the epiphany. Maybe she was what made me see that man in the mirror and realize it was time to get real and get ready for this conversation.

It likely wasn't only Nichole, but the entire dinner party that affected me. I was so moved by the experience of being there, and of seeing those older couples interact. Every time Mr. Blake called me *son*, I'd have to hold back the tears. It reminded me of my grandfathers, of my father, of all the men in my family who've passed, who once called me son. I was especially moved by the couples' conversation about our president and First Lady.

Listening to them talk about how they never thought they'd live long enough to see the United States elect a Black man as president reminded me of the journey we've all been through as Black people. It's one thing to talk about our achievements. It's another thing entirely to be sitting in the midst of people who helped shape that history, and to hear those men and women talk about how proud they are of someone from my generation—let alone someone I'd gone to school with and consider a friend.

There was a pride that I felt simply by being in the room. I'd felt that way before at rallies and concerts. I'd felt that way while listening to speeches by people like Dr. Martin Luther King, Jr., or Rev. Jesse Jackson or, more recently, President Obama. It's one of those feelings that makes you stand with your spine straight, makes you thankful for being Black, for being part of those people: the Black family.

What I felt in the Blakes' home was familial warmth of the sort that I hadn't felt since the last family reunion I'd attended. It made me remember my place in our history and our family. The reason I got sad in the midst of all that joy and love was that I couldn't bear to think of it—the Black family—as something that might soon belong solely to the past. I mean, look at us. Even among perfect strangers, we're able to acknowledge our familial ties, ties that are so binding that they've become part of our vernacular. We call each other "brotha" or "sistah" or even "blood," as in "Yo, blood, what's up?" If I'd wanted to skip the formalities when I walked into the Blake home and jump right in to calling Mr. Blake "Pops," I know that would have been acceptable. That's just how we do it.

As I was sitting there with them, I realized that I'd gotten lost without even noticing. The Black family is my home. It always has been. But I felt so far from any prospect of creating my own branch of it with a wife and child. I kept looking around and asking myself, *How did that happen?*

I've always been keenly aware of my desire and responsibility to help strengthen the Black family. I've always been committed to helping young Black kids recognize and respect their potential and the power of their legacies. By volunteering as a Big Brother, and by trying to mentor kids through literature, I hope to help them find their way back home and realize that they have a home and a family. I'm sure that my own desire to have a home, to find my way back, is what inspired me to buy that property in Colorado and reserve it, at least in my mind, for my own family gatherings and reunions. But I wasn't taking the necessary steps to transform the property from a house into the home that I'd envisioned.

I wonder whether the weight of all that awareness is what finally brought on the epiphany. The universe had delivered a woman to me who seemed to possess all the qualities I claimed to want. And yet there I was, walking away. Was it all of that that led me to the moment in the car? Or was it the moment in the car that led me to look back on those events and understand their meaning?

I suppose it doesn't really matter. What's done is done. There's fried chicken, and there's scrambled eggs. It doesn't matter which one came first. I'm here now, where I belong, on my way back home. I'm going to be a partner in building a strong, healthy, happy family. I am going to be a part of the solution, not a part of the problem. I am going to be a partner in building a home.

Nichole and I have been seeing each other for a few months now, and it already feels familiar and comfortable. It feels very right. She has got to be one of the most intelligent people I have ever met in my life. When I overhear her tutoring math or reviewing calculus homework with one of her students on the phone, she seems like a stranger from another world, speaking a language I don't understand. Of course, that only makes me admire her more. She can teach me things, and I, in turn, can teach her a thing or two as well.

Ordinarily, I would have written off any thought of a relationship with someone like Nichole, someone who makes her home clear across the country from where I make mine; someone who has an adolescent child; someone whose profession is completely different from mine. It's not that I wouldn't have been taken by Nichole; I would have been—I was . . . I am. But

I would've told myself from the start that it would not work, that there'd be no way the relationship would survive beyond a week or two, so why even bother?

In fact, I did tell myself that. I almost didn't call, even though I'd promised her I would. Even after I met Nichole, I spent so much time trying to figure out what she wanted, because at some level I was getting ready to tell her that I was not the one she should look to for those things. If we were to get together, I told myself, one of us would have to pack up our whole life and relocate. Was I willing to even consider that? We'd have to go through the difficult process of creating a place for me in her daughter's life—that is, if her daughter decided that she wanted me there to begin with.

I've had children around me my entire life, and because of my writing and volunteer work, I spend a great deal of time with adolescent kids. I love being around them. Still, they are at a safe distance. They will never call me "Dad."

The more I thought about Nichole, the more frightened I got. The fear was all in place before our first phone call. Ironically, I called her not because I managed to get past my fear, but because I didn't want to hurt her feelings by not calling. She had asked me a direct question—"Will you call?"—and I'd given her an answer. If I couldn't even make a commitment to calling someone and keep it, how could I ever make a commitment to loving someone for the rest of my life and expect to keep that? Besides, Nichole was friends with Don and Robin. If I shamed myself, I'd also be shaming them. So I called, and despite my fears and apprehensions, I've kept calling.

Now here we are. Nichole and I talk nearly every day. We are in a committed and monogamous relationship. And most important, we are building a pretty solid friendship. So far we've managed to see each other two or three times a month. I travel a lot, and if her schedule allows, she'll meet me wherever I might be. I've gone to see her in D.C. a few times, and she's come to L.A. a couple of times. She really is an amazing woman. Her picture is my screen saver, and every time I see her dark chocolate skin and almond brown eyes, I am reminded that Black women are the most beautiful women in the world. However, there was one piece of unfinished business that was making me very nervous.

When the time came, I was nervous about meeting Nichole's daughter, Jade. What would I say? What would she think of me? I knew from my own experience that kids whose parents are divorced always hold hope that one day their parents will get back together. The presence of another person in one of her parent's lives seemingly erases that possibility. I didn't want Jade to hate me just because I liked her mother.

I still wasn't sure why I was so filled with anxiety. My mind was racing and I needed to get some sleep on this red-eye to D.C. I usually find that the inconvenience of my anxiety is directly related to the seriousness of the subject I've sought to avoid.

When I finally fell asleep on the flight, a ghost came to visit me in my dreams. You know the Charles Dickens classic *A Christmas Carol,* where Scrooge is visited by the ghosts of Christmases past, present, and future? Well I was visited by the spirit of the biological daughter I hope to have one day once my family is started. She wanted to have *a conversation.*

Her appearance made me realize that it was not meeting Nichole's daughter that had me concerned (given who her mother was, I already knew the daughter would be delightful). Rather, my anxiety stemmed from what kind of relationship I would have with my own daughter when and if I had one.

I sat awake, wondering, Would all my mistakes and sins in my own relationships come back to haunt me in the form of having a daughter—or maybe more than one daughter—whom I would witness in their own relationships? This forced me to confront far more serious realities about my dealings with women than I wanted to remember. Those realities were not based just on my being "emotionally unavailable." Rather, my actions in relationships had hurt women that I loved and who loved me: spending the day with one woman and the night with another, being affectionate and then distant. It's one thing to catalogue your failings in relationships, but it's another to realize that one day you may have a young daughter who will date a version of you when you were at your worst. Oh, God.

I hope I have the courage to have that conversation with my future daughter and tell her about the man I'm not allowing myself to be anymore. From now on I am going to man up in my relationships with women and take care of their feelings the way I would want my future daughter's feelings cared for. It reminded me of an anonymous quote that someone had e-mailed me earlier that day. It read, "Spend time with your daughter, or someone else will."

As soon as I landed and met Jade, all my anxiety faded. She is as beautiful and poised as her mother. I treat her the way I treat all of the young people I meet while I'm volunteering or on book tours, and we get along great. I'm planning on taking her to Disneyland this summer when she's not in school.

You're probably thinking that I am doing really well in this relationship. At the very least, you're probably wondering how I was able to get over the fear and take the plunge; to allow myself to start falling for this woman in a way I'd never really fallen before. Well, the answer is that I am happier now with Nichole than I've ever been with any other woman. Nevertheless, I'm still as scared as I ever was. Instead of retreating, though, I try to advance through the fear. Sometimes it's with baby steps; other times it's by leaps and bounds. How'd I get myself to start doing that?

Prayer and a mantra.

Nichole and I pray together. She is the first woman I have ever been with where we take the time to pray for, about, and *with* each other. We even pray on the phone sometimes (of course . . . not during the sexy calls . . . but I call right back . . . lol). The strength of the spiritual bond that has come out of our prayers is like the plaster that is hardening the foundation of our friendship, setting the bricks of trust. With our joint elevation of faith comes the added joy of

> ❧
> **Three to be free.**
> ❧

patience, because we faithfully and fearlessly realize it is not our plan anyway. So, we give it to him and we are able to experience the ultimate lightness of being that God offers. There is no doubt that when prayers go up, blessings come down. And this beautiful Black queen is my great blessing here on earth. But it still takes work overcoming my fears.

To help, I came up with something of a mantra: three tenets to live by. They remind me of the clarity and resolve that I had during my epiphany. Most important, they free me from my fear and ground me, so that I can continue to move forward and allow myself to be happy in this relationship. They remind me to have an open and honest conversation—not only with myself but also with my partner. Those three tenets have become invaluable to me on this journey. I call them my "three to be free."

Number 1: Use the Past as a Guide, Not a Guarantee

The past is a double-edged sword. On the one hand, it's full of good memories and all the things we want to emulate. On the other hand, it can keep us frozen in place for fear of repeating a mistake or finding ourselves back in the same situation again.

The past can prejudice us against people, choices, actions, and lifestyles that we believe do not suit us. But not every situation is the same, and those people, choices, actions, and lifestyles may very well be precisely what we need.

I don't ever want to forget what we as Blacks have gone through—not the part about slavery; not the part about Jim Crow segregation; not the part about being liberated. All those parts of the journey are what make us who we are, and I am proud to be a part of that.

In August Wilson's play *Gem of the Ocean*, the character of Aunt Esther describes a "City of Bones," which is made up of the millions of bones of our ancestors that lie at the bottom of the Atlantic Ocean. Those bones are from the millions of slaves who were cast overboard and perished during the Middle Passage in four hundred years of slave trading. I never want to forget about the hardships and sacrifices endured by those who came before us, so that we might have the opportunity to build lives together as successful, happy, and healthy Black families.

There are also the images I don't necessarily want to remember but must—the lynchings and beatings, the separation and subjugation of Black families. These things don't just evaporate into thin air. They are memories and thoughts I will have for the rest of my life. They are memories and thoughts that we, as Black people, carry with us into our relationships with one another. I have chosen to use them as a guide, as a way for me to measure and celebrate how far we've come.

Past relationships are also tricky. While you can certainly learn from the mistakes—yours and your partners'—of past relationships, you have to remember that those are also only guides. Just because my ex-girlfriend started dating one of my closest male friends, I can't hold it against the women I meet in the future.

There is an old Native American saying that "you can't cross the same river twice." Nothing is the same, not even the water. The river you crossed the first time is no more. It's already rushed past you. My cousin Rev. Michael Bernard Beckwith of the Agape Center in Los Angeles always reminds me that fear is nothing more than an acronym: F.E.A.R.: false evidence appearing real.

The past provides us with evidence that appears real but might not be. It isn't a guarantee of anything except its own existence, in the past, with its own circumstances and explanations and context.

Number 2: If You Don't Mean It, Don't Say It

This is a big one.

How can you fault someone for expecting you to call when you're the one who promised to call in the first place? A lot of us, male and female, say things we don't mean and know the very moment we open our mouths that we have no intention of doing what we said we were going to do. It's amazing how these little white lies have become so commonplace in our society. We claim that it's to spare the other person's feelings, but I suspect it's to spare us from having to speak the truth and deal with the consequences.

A lot of us don't even stop to think of the other person's feelings. We don't think about the person we made the promise to, and their disappointment. Thanks to technology, we can text or e-mail our white lies now, instead of telling them face-to-face, where we would have to see the pain, anger, and hurt we caused.

I realize that there are times when we do have to tell white lies to actually spare someone's feelings, but surely not as many as we've got floating around today.

What I could never erase from my memory after I'd met Nichole was how open and vulnerable she'd allowed herself to be when she asked me if I'd call. I could see the sincerity of her emotion in her eyes. It made me feel horrible to think of the disappointment that I might have caused her had I not kept my word. I want to be able to give someone my word and have him or her know that I value it enough to keep it. I want people to be able to hold me to my word.

I'm also grateful to Don for stepping up and urging me to do the right thing by calling Nichole as I said I would. When you're not being loyal to who you really are, a true friend is someone who will be *courageous* enough to speak up. That also involves saying what you mean and meaning what you say.

Lately, I've been making every effort to think before I speak, to honor every word that comes out of my mouth. It's not easy. Try it, and you'll see just how hard it is. We tend to pick and choose which words or obligations we'll honor. When you pledge to do something, you're expected to uphold that commitment. It

> ❧
> I've been trying to honor every word that comes out of my mouth.
> ❧

feels like an onus only if your heart was never in it to begin with. Commitment is a promise that should be made with joy. When you say you're going to do something that you truly want to do, something that makes you happy, there's no reason why you wouldn't want to honor those words.

Number 3: Laugh, Dance, and Let Your Feelings Show

One of the things I most treasure about my friendship with Nichole is that we laugh a whole lot. She and I have so much fun together, even if it's just sitting around on the phone talking nonsense. I don't know where we got the idea that relationships had to become so serious after we grew up, but it's gotta go. I have a friend who always tries to move into apartments that are near schools. She says she loves to hear the children walking by her window.

"They're always giggling and so full of life," she said. "How do we end up losing that?" I don't know, but I don't think it's healthy. I love being silly and having Nichole laugh at me and with me. Laughter plays such a central role in our relationship. When she's not around, it's one of the things I look forward to doing with her. I will sometimes think of something funny or hear a joke, and my first impulse is to call her and share it with her because I want to hear her laugh. I want to laugh with her.

I'd forgotten that fun should exist in a relationship. I'd gotten so caught up in my past relationships with all the grown-up negotiations: What fancy restaurant should we go to for dinner tonight, can we pencil each other in for lunch on this day, and so forth. It seemed like everything was about business, business, business. There was no fun. A couple of weeks ago, I showed up at Nichole's door to hang out with her, and the first thing she did when she opened it was to squirt me with a water gun. Once I was in and had closed the door behind me, she threw me a water gun, letting me know that there was going to be a duel. We had our gunfight, and at the end of it we were both drenched. I haven't done anything like that since I was young—I mean since before high school.

But that's the kind of stuff we do. Her daughter plays the latest songs for us. I'm talking about the ones that aren't even on the radio yet, and we'll dance around the living room. Of all the things I thought I'd be doing at this age with my girlfriend, learning "da stanky legg" dance was not one of them. But I had a great time doing it, and the next time I did a speaking engagement with young people in the audience, they were so impressed when I threw in a sentence with "da stanky legg" dance in it. The whole crowd burst into laughter. Like I said earlier, lightness of being can be contagious.

Something else that used to really hold me in a place of fear was that I thought that if people knew how you felt about them, then they had the power to hurt you, and so I didn't let my girlfriends know how much I cared about them.

I realize that people are scared of vulnerability, but here's what's also true: If people know how you feel about them, it might just make them feel good. And it gives them the opportunity to let you know how they feel about you, which could make you feel good as well. Sure, there's the possibility that you could get hurt, but that wouldn't

> ❧
> It's not easy to free yourself from fear. It's not easy to trust someone and to love someone.
> ❧

change the fact that you still had feelings for that person. Why not take the chance and express those feelings? They're not doing anybody any good bottled up inside. Without Nichole's show of vulnerability, I might not have felt inspired or safe to let myself respond in kind, and we might not be together right now.

I won't lie: This journey has been hard work. It's not easy to free myself from fear. It's not easy to trust someone and to love someone. We all say we want it, but we become uncomfortable when it means that we have to grow, to bare our souls. But the reward is immediate and it's incredible. There is nothing that can compare to the power and the beauty of love, of allowing ourselves to love and be loved. There is a divinity to it.

I do believe that God and the universe have a wonderful and unreasonably happy life in store for us, but it's up to us to step into it. It starts with the way we speak to and about one another. I want all of us to embrace our vision of a future characterized by kindness, beauty, courage, laughter, and happiness, an intuitive knowledge that our lives don't have to look the way other people say they do. It's a courageous, smile-filled realization that we create our own reality. It's a conscious awareness that every time someone says, "There are no good—— out there," we respond with an energized, openhearted smile and say, "That's not true. There are plenty of really great—— out there for *me!*" Believe it! Know it! Create it! Claim it! Our future is divinely written and it is *amazing* and overflowing with *love!* We deserve it. We will have it. *Trust and believe.*

My models for that type of love were my grandparents: four Black people who were committed to their mates and to the forward motion of their community and their family. That's what feels like home to me, so that's what I want in my own life. If that's what you envision for your own life, it's time to take your own journey and to have "the conversation."

ADDENDUM: CONVERSATION QUESTIONS

Whether you ever have a Conversation Party or not, here are some questions you can ask yourself, your partner, or a group.

A LOOK IN THE MIRROR

If someone was watching you right now, what might his or her first impression of you be? (Are you smiling, frowning, how are you dressed, what are you doing, what type of energy are you giving off? . . .)

When you are among your peers, are there generally more positive comments made about Black men (or women), or more negative comments?

What is your personal temperament? How do you handle conflicts?

What is the best way for you to be approached when you are upset? The worst way?

Do you prefer to be single or to be in a relationship? What are the pros and cons of each?

Single people: Why are you single?

Do you believe in gender roles? Explain.

What is the longest time you have gone without being involved with someone in a way that was not strictly platonic? How was that time for you?

What additional experiences do you hope to have before this life is complete?

RELATIONSHIPS

What kind of people have you dated and why?

How do you feel about your relationship history? What have you learned from these experiences?

What are ideal qualities and physical attributes you want in a partner? List them.

What are your thoughts on the idea of a soul mate?

What example do you hope to leave on others of your own relationship?

What does a healthy relationship look like to you?

What do you think is the answer to achieving a healthy relationship? What personal advice would you give? Do you follow your own advice?

What are your relationship fears?

What gets on your nerves when you are dating or in a serious relationship?

Why do you think African American men and women are struggling to have successful relationships? What can you do to beat the odds?

What are your thoughts about platonic friendships between men and women? How can these friendships affect relationships?

Why do you think that some men can commit to one woman and not another?

What impact do you think entertainment media and technology have on relationships?

LOVE

How do you show love?

What lets you know you are loved?

What are the thoughts that come to mind when you hear the word "love"?

What is your definition of love?

Have you ever experienced love? What was it like?

How do you know when you are in love?

MARRIAGE

What are your thoughts about being engaged? When do you think is the right time to become engaged? How do you know that you are ready?

What do you think about marriage? Do you want to get married? Why?

What do you think it means to have a successful marriage?

What do you think are some of the challenges and rewards of being married?

How does your ideal long-term relationship look?

What do you hope to have meant to your partner's life?

SEX

What are your earliest memories of sex? How were you raised to think about sex?

How do you think your early childhood experiences have impacted the way you came to view sex both as a teenager and as an adult?

How would you describe yourself sexually? How would you describe your partner?

What have been some of your fantasies? Have you ever made them a reality? Why or why not?

Have you and your current partner discussed your individual sexual health histories? Why or why not?

KIDS

What concerns would you have dating somebody who already has children? How would you foresee overcoming these challenges?

Do you want children? If so, how many?

What are your personal parental philosophies on raising children? How would you discipline? What are your goals in raising kids?

What type of parent do you think you would be (or already are)?

What type of parent do you think your partner would be (or already is)?

MONEY

What concerns about money and relationships do you have?

What is your individual financial history? (How do you handle money? What is your credit like and why? Are you in debt?)

What are your thoughts about your partner's financial habits?

What are your thoughts on prenuptial agreements?

How do you think finances should be handled in a relationship? How many accounts would you ideally like to have?

What have been some of your biggest financial challenges? What have been some of your biggest financial accomplishments?

EXES

How do you feel about your mate connecting with their ex?

What are your relationships like with your ex partners?

What have your personal experiences been in dealing with your mate's exes?

CHEATING

What have your experiences been with infidelity? Have you ever cheated or been cheated on? What impact have these experiences played in your life?

What is your definition of cheating? Have you discussed this with your significant other?

Would you be able to overcome infidelity in a relationship? Why or why not?

Why do you think people cheat?

FAITH

What is your religious and spiritual background?

What role has religion/spirituality played in your life and what are your current personal thoughts, experiences, and beliefs?

What role do you think religious/spiritual beliefs play in a relationship?

What do you think of relationships where there are two different religious backgrounds? Could you be in one? Why or why not?

What are your thoughts on interracial relationships?

HEALTH/STDS

Have you ever had an STD? How did it affect your life?

When was the last time you were tested for all STDs? Have you ever discussed your sexual history with your partners?

What are your thoughts about going to therapy? What are your thoughts about going to therapy with your mate?

ACKNOWLEDGMENTS

God is the creator of all things and when it comes to expressing the gratitude in my heart, for me, that is where it begins.

Oscar Wilde once said that "the smallest act of kindness is worth more than the grandest intention," and as I complete my third book, I would like to acknowledge those individuals whose unselfish and noble actions allowed me to be who I am today.

Since this book is entitled *The Conversation* I guess it was only appropriate that I had numerous "conversations," some formal and some not so formal, with so many friends and colleagues about the issues discussed in the book. Their insight and help can be seen throughout these pages. I want to acknowledge all of my family, friends, and colleagues who helped me flesh out my ideas, and gave me new perspectives and concepts to think about during the early versions of the book. They all offered constructive, encouraging, and helpful criticism to push my goal and vision forward. I also thank them for challenging me to not just discuss these issues from a theoretical or academic standpoint, but rather, pushed me to be vulnerable and speak to these issues from a personal point of view. To say this book of conversations has been a team effort would be an understatement. So I thank you all!

As we all know, silent gratitude isn't much use to anyone, so I humbly and profusely send a heartfelt thank you and expression of gratitude to the women I have dated and had relationships with during the course of my life, most of whom, I am proud to say, I am still friends with to this day. I consider myself one of the luckiest men in the world because I have had in my life amazingly intelligent, talented, and beautiful women who continue to inspire and challenge me.

This project could not have been done without my very talented friend Meri Nana-Ama Danquah and all of her help and commitment with this book. To my analytical and inquisitive friend, Samantha Dixon, for her amazing and exemplary work this year. My dear friend and fellow author, Stephanie Convington—thanks for understanding and simply being there when I needed you.

To Ben ("Don") Watkins, thank you for contributing your thoughts, experiences, and wisdom to this book. And to Dr. Tanya Martin, for taking the time to offer your expertise and training.

At this point in my life, I understand what William Feather meant when he said "something that has always puzzled me all my life is why, when I am in special need of help, the good deed is usually done by somebody on whom I have no claim," and this is true when it comes to many things in my life, specifically this book. To my amazing staff: Danielle Caldwell, who worked tirelessly and contributed greatly to the completion of my most challenging work to date—thanks for being the multitalented, sweet, and loving person you are; and Darrell Smith, who is always there to help whenever and however possible. Their help can be seen throughout the pages of this book. To the superb Cynne Simpson, Brett Mahoney, Kathy Busby and Matt McGough, Nzingha Clarke, Jennifer Cohns Beugleman, Ari Palitz, Emily Nelson, Nillah Turrentine and Valeisha Butterfield, Marvet Britto and everyone at the Britto Agency, thanks for your terrific insight.

And heartfelt thanks to William Shinker, Lauren Marino, Brianne Ramagosa, and everyone at Gotham/Penguin who have helped shape this book. Thanks to my friend, the oh-so-talented and incomparable Chris Mann. To Gilda Squire, Celessa Batchan, Nyanza Shaw, and Karen Lewis Farrelly—thank you for your time and hard work.

A very special thanks to my mother, Marilyn Hill Harper, for your undying love and support on all things that I have done and continue to do. I would thank you from the bottom of my heart, but for you my heart has no bottom.

And finally, thanks to Him from whom all blessings flow— without the guidance, love, and support from my Creator—this creation would not exist.

Peace and abundant blessings to all.